On
Personality

This is a really excellent book, one that (for once) may truly claim to be 'accessible to someone with no technical philosophical knowledge' and yet philosophically meaty enough to be of interest not only to philosophy undergraduates but even to specialists . . . The style is delightful . . . the humour engaging . . . and the chapters beautifully balanced.

Rosalind Hursthouse, author of *On Virtue Ethics*

Praise for the series

'. . . allows a space for distinguished thinkers to write about their passions'

The Philosophers' Magazine

'. . . deserve high praise'

Boyd Tonkin, *The Independent* (UK)

'This is clearly an important series. I look forward to reading future volumes.'

Frank Kermode, author of *Shakespeare's Language*

'both rigorous and accessible'

Humanist News

'the series looks superb'

Quentin Skinner

'. . . an excellent and beautiful series'

Ben Rogers, author of *A.J. Ayer: A Life*

'Routledge's *Thinking in Action* series is the theory junkie's answer to the eminently pocketable Penguin 60s series.'

Mute Magazine (UK)

'Routledge's new series, *Thinking in Action*, brings philosophers to our aid . . .'

The Evening Standard (UK)

'. . . a welcome new series by Routledge'

Bulletin of Science, Technology and Society (Can)

PETER GOLDIE

On
Personality

Routledge
Taylor & Francis Group

LONDON AND NEW YORK

First published 2004
by Routledge
11 New Fetter Lane, London EC4P 4EE

Simultaneously published in the USA and Canada
by Routledge
29 West 35th Street, New York, NY 10001

Routledge is an imprint of the Taylor & Francis Group

Typeset in Joanna MT and DIN by
RefineCatch Ltd, Bungay, Suffolk
Printed and bound in Great Britain by
TJ International Ltd, Padstow, Cornwall

British Library Cataloguing in Publication Data
A catalogue record for this book is available from the British Library

Library of Congress Cataloging in Publication Data
Goldie, Peter.
   On personality/Peter Goldie. – 1st edn
      p.   cm. – (Thinking in action)
   1. Personality. 2. Character. I. Title. II. Series.
   BD331.G585   2004
126 – dc22   2003026287

ISBN 0-415-30513-6 (hbk)
ISBN 0-415-30514-4 (pbk)

Preface

There are many people to thank. I benefited greatly from the comments, remarks and intuitions of the students who attended lectures and seminars on various topics which bear on this book. My colleagues in the Philosophy Department of King's College London kindly took on my duties for a sabbatical term, during which I worked on this book, partly here in London, and partly in South Africa at Rhodes University. During my stay in South Africa, Deane-Peter Baker, Simon Beck, Ward Jones, Tom Martin, Francis Williamson, Marius Vermaak, Sam Vice and many others made me welcome; they all helped too in all sorts of ways, with suggestions, ideas, guidance, drinks. Ward Jones and Adam Morton read and commented on the whole manuscript. Matt Cavanagh, Geraldine Hamilton, Sophie Hamilton, Ian Hislop, Pam Joll and Stewart Wood made suggestions and provided examples, as did many others, some perhaps less aware that this was what they were doing. Adam Morton, Keith Oatley and David Velleman helped by exchanging emails, letting me see their unpublished material, and more widely. Tony Bruce and his colleagues at Routledge were very efficient and professional, and Tony encouraged me and made lots of suggestions. The support of Bernard Williams, who died last year, goes back a long way. Two colleagues at King's, M. M. McCabe and David Papineau, have shown great friendship.

Peter Goldie
London
2004

One

PERSONALITY DISCOURSE IS EVERYWHERE

Not all the officers in the fleet were as pleased as Nelson to hear of Jervis's appointment. [Sir John Jervis was appointed as commander of the Mediterranean Fleet in 1796.] There was an air of menace about him. With his powerful frame and stern features, he looked, as he could be, a formidable opponent. He had a reputation as a firm disciplinarian, and, as a man who knew him well said, he was far from always 'preserving an unruffled command of his temper'. When roused 'a torrent of impetuous reproof in unmeasured language would violently rush from his unguarded lips'. 'He had, too, a certain grim humour in which he occasionally indulged at the expense of those who were powerless to retort. On the other hand, when an act of zeal, skill or gallantry merited his approval, it was given ungrudgingly . . . and in his private relations, though careful and economical, he was kindhearted and generous.'[1]

Wherever you find people, thinking, talking and writing about other people, there you'll find discourse about personality – about, as the *Oxford English Dictionary* has it, 'that quality or assemblage of qualities which makes a person what he is, as distinct from other persons'.[2] We call people kindhearted, generous, fair-minded, witty, flaky, charming, mean-spirited, bitchy, dull, stupid, thoughtless, self-deprecating, bullies, control freaks. Aspects of personality such as these, or what I will call *traits* (which I pronounce to rhyme with 'baits' rather than with 'bays'), are constantly being appealed to in our everyday descriptions of ourselves and of others.

Ask a friend of yours to describe a mutual friend who is absent, or someone she knows from the place where she works, but with whom you are not acquainted. Listen to what she says, and you are almost bound to hear talk of traits.

Look at any recent advertisement in the lonely-hearts or personal column of your newspaper or magazine: John describes himself as caring, passionate, fun to be with; Adrienne is warm, funny and attractive, and seeks a kind, confident, intelligent man with laughter lines. Look at job specifications: 'Successful applicants will be enthusiastic, ambitious, competitive, determined, energetic and outgoing.'

The newspapers are full of talk of personality traits: politicians are described as being charismatic, charming and professional, or dogged and shallow. Footballers are hardworking or mercurial. In the law courts, judges and magistrates don't hesitate to talk about the criminal's personality as they pass sentence: this evil man revealed that he was cunning, ruthless and devious in the pursuit of his terrible deeds.

Historians write about the personality of their historical characters: in the Christopher Hibbert book on Nelson which I just quoted from, the index entry under 'Nelson, personality' has page references to where the following traits, amongst many others, are revealed in action: 'courage', 'determination', 'self-esteem', 'self-confidence', 'hatred of the French', 'taciturnity', 'tactlessness', 'foolhardiness', 'short temper', 'pugnacity', 'generosity', 'complacency', 'vanity', 'courtesy', and 'fondness of children'. And under 'Emma, Lady Hamilton, personality' we have 'good nature', 'charm', 'self-confidence', 'need for admiration', 'sensuality' and 'extravagance'.

In novels, short stories, films and TV soaps and cartoons, some characters are drawn with such clear, sharp lines that the character's name becomes a word to describe a personality trait: we can gain a nice idea of someone's personality if you say that he or she is a Homer Simpson, a Micawber, a Walter Mitty, a Pollyanna, a Bertie Wooster, a Gordon Gekko, an Oblomov or a Runyonesque type, and we know what you mean even if we've never read or seen the work that the character comes from. These are E. M. Forster's 'flat characters' who, at the extreme, can be summed up in a single sentence.[3] For obvious reasons, the names of more complex characters in novels (Forster's 'round' characters) are seldom used in this way: for example, if you were to say of someone that he's a Pierre Bezukhov (one of the central characters of *War and Peace*), it would tell us nothing about him – or rather it would tell us too much. Whereas, if you say that he's a bit of a Walter Mitty, you can be readily understood as meaning that he's someone who lives in a fantasy world of his own making; and if you say that she's a Pollyanna, you mean that she always looks on the bright side of life. Sometimes, the folk memory of historical characters becomes such that they too are left with just one defining aspect to their personality; the rest is, so to speak, whited out: he's a bit of a Genghis Khan; she's a Florence Nightingale.

WHY IS IT EVERYWHERE?

Personality discourse is everywhere largely because it serves a purpose: or rather, because it serves several purposes. We use personality discourse to describe people, to judge them, to enable us to predict what they will think, feel and do, and to enable us to explain their thoughts, feelings and actions. Let's take these in turn.

If I say that Aubrey is outgoing, and that Briony is a shy person, I'm saying something about them: I'm attributing a certain personality trait to them. Sometimes we can do this obliquely, by implication, without actually using a trait term. I ask you what sort of person Gideon is, and you reply 'Well, he is a litigation lawyer.' On the assumption that you are not changing the subject by telling me about what Gideon does for a job, I can take it that you are implying that Gideon has the sort of personality that is the image of a typical litigation lawyer (like the character played by Dan Hedaya in *Clueless*, the father of Alicia Silverstone's Cher Horowitz).

In describing someone by reference to a personality trait, I might also be judging him or her. This kind of judgement might be only in respect of some project or plan or task in hand. If you are recruiting a trainee in media sales for your office, then Aubrey's outgoingness will better qualify him for the job than Briony's shyness. In selecting a football team, one might prefer that a defender be hardworking rather than mercurial.

A character trait is deeper than a personality trait, and the judgement goes deeper too. Knowing that Gideon is cruel and that Susan is kind reveals something more profound about them than that they are charming or quick-witted. It reveals something about them that we are rightly inclined to say is concerned with their *moral worth as a person*. Being cruel is a morally bad thing about someone, and being kind is a morally good thing.

Our present conception of personality has really only emerged since the eighteenth century (this sense of the term

dates from then), and it is perhaps a peculiarly modern phenomenon to attach such importance to the superficialities of
personality and mere appearances (charm, charisma, 'being a
personality'), but scratch the surface and you'll find that we
all still have an underlying idea of character which goes back
at least as far as the ancient Greeks, and which is wonderfully
expressed by Aristotle. Personality, in the modern superficial
sense, hasn't *supplanted* our idea of character. One might say
that the doubts many people felt about President Clinton,
after various personal scandals beset his presidency, were
doubts about his character; no one doubted his personality,
his charm, his ability to 'work' an audience. Character, in this
sense, will be the central topic of Chapter 2.

And we use trait discourse to help us to predict things
about people. Adrienne advertises in the lonely-hearts for a
kind, confident, intelligent man because she wants a man
with these traits, and because she thinks that a man with these
traits will reliably think, feel and act in a kind, confident and
intelligent way. I will say more about this shortly.

So we describe, judge and predict by using personality
discourse. And finally, we use personality discourse to
explain. Freddie is your new boss. You go into his office to ask
him a question, and he shouts at you and humiliates you.
After crawling out, with his horrid words ringing in your
ears, you ask someone by the coffee machine why Freddie
should have done such a thing. 'Because he's a bully', comes
the reply. You feel better. You can rest assured that it isn't
something about *you* that caused Freddie to act as he did.
Moreover, the reply implies that it isn't something that is
particular to Freddie's state of mind *today* or *this week*. Rather,
the implication of the reply to your question is that
this behaviour is *characteristic* of Freddie. You now have this

description of Freddie ('he's a bully'). You can make a judgement of him as a boss ('lousy', 'thoroughly demotivating'), and as a person ('bad', 'exploitative'), and you condemn him for being the way he is. You can predict what he'll do the next time you go into his office to ask him a question. And the next time you go into his office, you'll be able to explain why he did what you predicted he'd do. Freddie himself might say that his behaviour has this characteristic pattern because 'they keep sending me these useless, ignorant new trainees, who are always bothering me with trivial questions'. But *we* know better.

Or do we? There is a popular view in social psychology, and in philosophy, that personality traits are much less robustly reliable than we ordinarily think, and that we are far too quick in our trait attributions, often on very paltry evidence. Some even deny that there are personality traits at all. This is a topic of Chapter 3, and here, in this chapter, I will pretty much take for granted our ordinary, everyday view: that personality discourse is everywhere for the good reasons that I have been discussing.

Now I want to head towards saying what personality is. In doing this, I will try to capture our everyday idea of, or concept of, a personality trait. Doing this sort of thing – sometimes called conceptual analysis – is an important starting point for many philosophical enterprises. What ought to emerge is an account that we can all pretty much agree on – after all, it's meant to be 'common sense', so we all ought to be talking about the same thing (allowing for some disagreement at the edges). Remember, though, that capturing our concept of something doesn't tell us whether there is in reality anything that our concept is a concept of. We have a pretty clear concept of a witch and of a unicorn, but it is a question of empirical fact whether this world contains any witches or unicorns. Conceptual analysis alone cannot answer this question.

WHAT'S IN OUR MINDS?

Much of what is in our minds at any one time is relatively fleeting: at this moment I'm looking at the white van that is double-parked in the street outside my house; I feel slightly hungry; I'm still angry with my son at his rudeness over breakfast; I have a slight ache in my right knee; the van driver's shirt reminds me that David Beckham now plays for Real Madrid; I'm thinking about my trip to South Africa. Let's call these relatively fleeting aspects of my mind *occurrent* thoughts and feelings: they come and go.

Then there are other aspects of our minds which are relatively enduring. Let's call these *states* – to capture the idea that they are not in flux. I love my son (in spite of feeling angry with him at the moment); I have a special liking for the best, most mature Parmesan cheese; I have an enduring aversion to what are known as 'flat hats'. These psychological states are not in the forefront of my mind at all times – I'm not always aware of them. I am, however, likely to become aware of them, and to act on them, when the occasion arises: when my son gives me that humorous look; when there is some really special Parmesan in the shop window in front of me; when someone wearing a flat hat comes into view.

So far, I think, we don't have an example of a personality trait. Intuitively, a personality trait is relatively enduring – it's a kind of state – so that eliminates my *occurrent* thoughts and feelings as candidates. But the relatively stable states of mind that I have mentioned so far, such as an aversion to flat hats, are I think, too *particular* in what they are about.

Let's now assume that I have an aversion not only to flat hats, but also to all sorts of other things that one is likely to find in the English countryside: muddy roads, sheep and cattle, fields, tea shops with no espresso, villages with no cinemas, and so on. Given that I have this aversion, you can rely on me to steer away from the countryside, and if I have to be away from the big city for some reason, you can be confident that I'll do my best to get back as soon as possible. Now I think we have an example of a personality trait: I'm a *town person*, a *townie* – someone who prefers the town to the countryside.

Similarly, assume that I don't just prefer the best Parmesan but generally prefer the very best kinds of food. Then I'm a *foodie*. And if I have loving thoughts and feelings towards people in general (and not just my son) then I'm a *loving person*. So being a town person, a foodie and a loving person are personality traits; in other words, they can be part of someone's personality.

Spend a bit more time looking at these examples. Take being a foodie: having an enduring state of mind which is, roughly, an enduring preference for the best kinds of food. This enduring preference is a *disposition* – a disposition to have certain kinds of occurrent thoughts and feelings about food, and to act in certain characteristic ways. For example, it involves the following dispositions: to choose the best kinds of food; to look out for, and go to, restaurants that cater to my taste; to think that money spent on the best kinds of food is money well spent; to feel a special pleasure when I taste really good food; to avoid transport cafés and McDonald's; and so on.

I need now to say briefly what I mean in general by a disposition, for it will be central to the whole discussion of personality.

SUGAR, VASES, POULTICES AND MUSHROOMS

All sorts of things have dispositions. A sugar cube is soluble. Its being soluble (its solubility) is a disposition of the sugar cube. A glass vase is fragile. Its being fragile (its fragility) is a disposition of the vase. Dispositions like these can be understood in terms of what I will call 'if–then' *conditional statements*. To say that this sugar cube is soluble means, roughly, that if it is immersed in a warm fluid, then it will (can be expected to) dissolve. This glass vase is fragile: if it is dropped, then it will break. The mustard poultice alleviates pain: if it is applied to the painful area, then it will alleviate the pain (note that we don't always have a single word to name a disposition). So things have dispositions even when the circumstances in the 'if' part of the 'if–then' conditional don't obtain: the glass vase is fragile even when it's sitting safely on the mantelpiece.

We might or might not know what are the underlying properties of the thing that *explain* the disposition that it has. We have a pretty good idea of what are the underlying structural properties of a sugar cube and a vase that will explain their being soluble and fragile. But (I understand) we don't know what the properties of a poultice are that explain its disposition to alleviate pain. However, whether or not we know about the underlying explanatory properties, knowing that something has a disposition of a certain kind can itself be useful in our practical lives. That's why we have so many concepts of dispositions.

You visit a strange country and are told by the locals that the mushrooms that are plentiful in their forests are poisonous. Even if you have no idea of why they are poisonous, it's still extremely useful to know that if you eat one, then you'll be very ill.

Of course, these mushrooms' being poisonous (their

having that particular disposition) isn't an *explanation* of why, if you eat them, you'll be very ill, because something's being poisonous just *is* its being such that, if you eat it, then you'll be very ill. This kind of non-explanation is sometimes called by philosophers a *dormative virtue* explanation, after Molière's mockery of eighteenth-century doctors in his *La Malade Imaginaire*: when the doctors were asked why opium induces sleep, they replied that it did so because of its dormative virtues; or rather, to disguise the non-explanatoriness in a cloak of Latin, they said that it did so because of its *virtus dormativa*.

But still, in a different context, appeal to dispositions can be explanatory. For example, if we notice that all the tourists on the coach get ill after eating these mushrooms, it's an explanation of their getting ill to say that it's because the mushrooms that they ate are poisonous. Some philosophers say that this is just a shallow explanation, because it doesn't explain *why* the mushrooms are poisonous – what it is about them (their chemical structure perhaps) that is the ground of this disposition. Maybe, but often, as is the case in this imagined example, it's the best we've got, and can be the place to begin the search for a deeper explanation.

CHARM, GLOOMINESS AND IRASCIBILITY

Personality traits are dispositions. Just as this mushroom, whilst nestling amongst the leaves of the forest, is poisonous, so James, whilst asleep on the sofa in front of the TV, is charming, friendly, patient, cheerful, slow-witted and good at dancing. Because personality traits are dispositions, for each personality trait there will be some kind of an 'if–then' conditional.

But to say what the 'if–then' conditional looks like for personality traits in *general* is, I think, a hopeless task, because they are so disparate in kind. History is littered with failed personality theories, largely because of their seriously mistaken attempts to regiment personality traits, often into a given number of neat pigeon-holes. There were the four humours of Hippocrates: blood, black bile, yellow bile and phlegm. The Roman physician Galen thought that any of these in excess gave you one of four possible temperaments: sanguine, melancholic, choleric or phlegmatic. These days we have extraversion and introversion or neuroticism, and the 'five-factor' model: neuroticism, extraversion, openness, agreeableness and conscientiousness.[4] So, studiously avoiding any excessive theorising or regimenting, here are some broad kinds of personality trait, many of which overlap and merge into each other, so that it's not always obvious into which kind any given personality trait falls.

(a) Ways of acting

Examples are being charming and being polite. Roughly, these traits are ways of doing things. A charming person will invite you to her party in a charming way, and will speak to you over dinner in a charming way. A polite person will pass the salt politely, and come into the room politely. This isn't to suggest that these people will manifest their traits on all occasions when they can; it's sometimes said (in jest of course) that an English gentleman can be rude sometimes, but when he is, you can be sure that it's intentional.

(b) Habits

Being fidgety is a habit. Roughly, a habit is a tendency to repeat a certain kind of action or bodily movement, often without realising that this is what you are doing. A fidgety person might rattle the change in his pocket or fiddle with the knot to his tie, or tap his feet under the table.

(c) Temperaments

Being cheerful, being phlegmatic (residues of Galen), being nervous and being gloomy are temperaments. They are more embedded and more enduring than are moods, which can come and go. And they are more to do with feelings than are habits or ways of acting, although they can involve tendencies to act in certain characteristic ways. Gloomy Eeyore feels gloomy about his birthday and about the prospect of yet more festivities, thinks gloomily that it's bound to rain for the fireworks, plays gloomily with his presents, and so on.

(d) Emotional dispositions

An emotional disposition, such as irascibility and being envious, is a disposition to have a certain kind of emotion, often more (or less) than is appropriate, and to act out of that emotion. Emotional dispositions can be vices. Mr Angry is irascible, and gets angry with all sorts of silly things when he shouldn't, shouting at people, breaking vases, kicking the dog, slamming the car door.

(e) Enduring preferences and values

We've already looked at these. Foodies are disposed to think about and pursue good food in characteristic ways. Townies are disposed to think about and pursue/avoid the town/country in characteristic ways. Book-lovers seek out books, talk about books, save up to buy books, and so on.

(f) Skills, talents and abilities

Examples are being good at dancing, having a good ear for music, being a good carpenter or mathematician, being quick-witted. They are, roughly, capacities (a capacity is a kind of disposition) to perform certain tasks well. Some of these are 'natural'; others may take practice and training.

(g) Character traits

Character traits are importantly different from other aspects of personality. As I said earlier, character is deeper, personality more superficial, concerned with surface – I'll say what I mean by 'deeper' in Chapter 2. The etymology of personality suggests veneer, appearance: it's connected with the Latin word *persona*, a mask of the kind that used to be worn by actors; character emerges when the mask is removed.

All character traits are *reason-responsive*, whilst only some personality traits are. By this I mean that a character trait involves a disposition reliably to respond to certain kinds of reasons – unlike a mere action-tendency, behavioural habit or temperament, like being charming, or being fidgety or being gloomy. Consider, for example, kindness and vanity.

KINDNESS AND VANITY

Actions are done for reasons – reasons in the psychological sense, by which I mean occurrent thoughts and feelings. These thoughts and feelings may or may not be conscious, in the sense that the person doing the action needn't be aware of his or her reasons at the time of doing the action. In order to explain why someone did some action or other, we need to know what his or her reasons were.

Susan, seeing Miranda slip and drop her books in the street, goes up to her and helps her pick up her books. This is an action of Susan's, done for reasons. What were they? Let's say they were as follows: Susan saw that Miranda needed help, she felt sorry for Miranda, she wanted to help her, and she thought that picking up Miranda's books would be the best way of helping her in the circumstances. We can summarise these reasons for her action by saying that her motive was one of *kindness*, and that her action was kind.

This use of the term 'motive' in the singular doesn't imply that her act of kindness was done for a *single* reason. The term 'motive' works here in the way that a detective uses it when she wonders what the murderer's motive was: was it financial gain, jealousy, revenge? It's possible, in fact, for someone to do an action that can be properly classified as being kind – as being an action done out of a motive of kindness – without the notion of kindness *as such* featuring in her reasons at all; Susan needn't, for example, have the thought 'this would be the kind thing to do'. All we need is that Susan's reasons – of which there could be many – can be accurately said by us to be characteristic of kindness.

We can thus contrast Susan's action, done out of a motive of kindness, with the action of Augustus, who also stopped to help Miranda pick up her books, but who did this in order to curry favour with Miranda. We need not deny that Augustus helped Miranda, for indeed he did, but we should deny that Augustus' action was a kind one, for his motive was selfish or self-interested and not kind.[5]

So far I've only discussed Susan's motive, her occurrent thoughts and feelings, and not her character, her disposition. Susan might have a kind motive for helping Miranda without being a kind person. She might have just happened to have heard some good news about her pregnancy test, and when she saw Miranda drop her books, in a rare fit of bonhomie, she did something most unlike her – she helped someone. Susan's action would then have been done for kind reasons, or out of a motive of kindness, but she wouldn't be a kind person. To be a kind person she must have a relatively enduring disposition *reliably* to have kind motives and to act in a kind way, so that the appropriate 'if–then' conditional can be applied to her: roughly, if Susan is in a situation where kindness is appropriate, *then* she will reliably have thoughts and feelings that are characteristic of kindness, and thus will reliably act as a kind person should. It's in this sense that kindness, a character trait, is reliably reason-responsive.

The 'reliably' is important here. The term implies that we can have a reasonably high degree of confidence that Susan will be kind when she should. But it doesn't imply that we can *guarantee* that she will be kind whenever she should be. (This will be central to my discussion of the fragility of character in Chapter 3.)

Kindness is a good character trait, a virtue. The same sort of account I've just given can be applied to a bad character trait, a vice. Consider vanity. Arnold has spent the last hour in the gym constantly preening himself in the mirror and checking how he looks as he goes through his workout, striving to show his athletic figure off to the best effect. Why is Arnold doing these things? He's doing them out of vanity, although, as we have seen with kindness, this doesn't imply (which would be very unlikely anyway) that one of his reasons was 'doing this would be the vain thing to do'. Arnold's vanity, for vain is what he is, is his disposition in certain kinds of situation reliably to have certain kinds of occurrent thoughts and feelings (on this occasion, thoughts like 'Don't I look great with my pectorals all pumped up!'), and thus reliably to act in certain kinds of ways (on this occasion, doing actions like standing sideways on to see in the mirror how pumped up his pectorals are).

UNITY AND DIVERSITY

Politeness, being fidgety, cheerfulness, irascibility, being quick-witted, being a book-lover, kindness, vanity: these examples bring out the diverse nature of personality traits (here including character traits in this broader category). It's because of this diversity that it's so difficult to provide a definition of personality that is both true and reasonably succinct. But I hope that, in spite of this, what I've said about our everyday idea of personality meets your intuitions, at least about the central cases, even if there is some disagreement at the margin. There will be various qualifications that I'll need to make as I go along. Two I should mention now, although they will both come up again later.

First, some of our trait terms refer not to a disposition but to the *lack* of a disposition. Inconsiderateness, inhospitableness and thoughtlessness are like this. If we say of someone that she is inconsiderate, we are in effect saying that she is not considerate – that she lacks consideration for others. (If she were the sort of person who went out of her way to make sure that other people's lives went badly, then she would be something worse than inconsiderate.) Ruthlessness, on the other hand, *is* a disposition: it's a disposition to have *bad* kinds of occurrent thoughts and feelings, and thus to act badly in certain ways. So ruthlessness isn't just a lack of ruth. The surface grammar of our trait vocabulary can be misleading here – negative trait terms (inconsiderateness, ruthlessness) may refer to a trait or to a lack of a trait.

My second point is not so much a qualification as a comment or a pointer to one of the central themes of this book.

Nowhere have I said that a personality trait need be fixed, not open to change. Agreed, personality traits are relatively enduring (you can't become a kind person when you start your Weetabix and cease to be a kind person by the time you've finished your toast). But being relatively enduring is not the same as being fixed, not open to change. Our personality, including our deeply held traits of character as well as our more superficial traits, is capable of changing over time. This idea of a personality that can evolve, or even of one that can dramatically change through a kind of conversion (St Augustine), is related to what I will call the narrative sense of self. This is the topic of Chapter 5.

THE GOOD AND THE BEAUTIFUL, THE BAD AND THE UGLY

Often, talk of someone's personality is mixed up with talk of other attributes of the person that are, intuitively, nothing to do with personality as such. Here, for example, is a description of Joseph Goebbels in Ian Kershaw's masterful biography of Hitler:

> Possessed of a sharp mind and biting wit, the future Propaganda Minister, among the most intelligent of the leading figures in the Nazi Movement, had joined the NASDAP [the Nazi Party] at the end of 1924. Brought up in a Catholic family of moderate means . . . his deformed right foot exposed him from childhood days to jibes, taunts, and lasting feelings of physical inadequacy. That his earlier pretensions as a writer met with little recognition further fostered his resentment . . . His inferiority complex produced driving ambition and the need to demonstrate achievement through mental agility in a movement which derided both physical weakness and 'intellectuals'. Not least, it produced ideological fanaticism.[6]

Kershaw intermingles, with personality talk, talk of Goebbels' physical characteristics, his family background, his successes and failures, and so on. And this is quite usual, as novels, histories, lonely-hearts columns, obituaries and so on bear witness. Are these other attributes anything to do with personality? A moment's reflection should lead us to say yes. All sorts of attributes of a person can have a bearing on that individual's personality. But just *how* and *in what way* this works is interesting and revealing.

Right at the beginning of this chapter I mentioned a lonely-hearts ad in which Adrienne wrote that she wanted a man with laughter lines. Perhaps she just thought that laughter lines look nice on a man, like brown hair and blue eyes. But more likely she wanted a man with laughter lines because she thought that someone with laughter lines would also be someone who laughs a lot, and she wanted someone who laughs a lot. Very reasonable of her. When we meet people for the first time we look hard at their faces, because their faces – especially with age – bear the marks of their personality. Someone who frowns frequently, and whose lip is twisted into a permanent sneer, will have, after a time, these gestures frozen on her face. As Proust said: 'The features of our face are hardly more than gestures which force of habit has made permanent. Nature, like the destruction of Pompeii, like the metamorphosis of a nymph, has arrested us in an accustomed movement.'[7] We have a voracious appetite for studying these features. This is for a very good reason: not because these features are of interest in their own right (although they often are), but because they enable us to know *what the person is like* – they enable us to 'size up' a person.

So this is one way in which someone's personality trait can have a correlation with his or her physical attributes: the physical attribute (the laughter line, the fixed frown) is caused by regular expression of the trait, rather in the way that the regular crashing waves of the sea will, over time, cause the rocks on the seashore to have a certain shape.

A second kind of correlation is where we observe the behaviour, or what the behaviour causes, and this is itself an expression of the trait. A loud, braying voice reveals an unpleasant assertiveness. A tidily kept desk reveals conscientiousness. A video and DVD collection reveals a romantic streak. The choice of Pugin wallpaper reveals ostentatiousness.

A third kind of correlation is like the second, but with an added twist. Here, someone aspires to have a trait, and then acts, acquires possessions and so on, in ways that give the impression that he already has the trait. A young man aspires to be a sort of man-about-town, a Bertie Wooster type. Because he thinks it goes with being this sort of toff, he buys a pair of those slippers with his initials embroidered on them that you can get in Jermyn Street, just off Piccadilly. He wants us to think he's a man-about-town; in fact we think he's pretentious.

This reveals something very important about development of one's personality. One of the many horrible things about being young, and especially about being a teenager, is that we don't really know who we are. Of course we know who we are in one sense (barring amnesia, being a foundling and the like), but we don't know what *sort of a person* we are. At that age we tend to try on styles of clothes to see which ones are 'right' for us. And we also tend, metaphorically speaking, to 'try on' various kinds of personality (Bart Simpson 'trying on' being cool). Perhaps after a time, what this young man has been trying on – his slippers and his personality – sticks: his slippers and his personality become just as much a part of who he is – of what sort of a person he is – as the traits that he had as a child. Once he was pretentious, now he really is a Bertie Wooster type, living it out in all sorts of ways: rising at ten-thirty, avoiding work at all costs, as well as wearing those ghastly slippers. As Nietzsche said, 'If someone obstinately and for a long time wants to *appear* something it is in the end hard for him to *be* anything else. The profession of almost every man, even that of the artist, begins with hypocrisy, with an imitation from without, with a copying of what is most effective.'[8]

So far I've been considering physical characteristics which reveal or are expressive of a personality trait (the laughter lines, the braying voice, the wallpaper, the slippers). Sometimes the causal process can work in the other direction, so that a physical characteristic can have a causal influence on the development of the trait. So not only does personality affect appearances, appearances can affect personality; as Oscar Wilde said, 'it is only shallow people who do not judge by appearances. The true mystery of the world is the visible, not the invisible.' For example, there is some evidence that taller people tend to be more dominant than people of average height: not because height and dominance are directly correlated, but because taller people tend to stand out in a crowd, and get noticed. And Ian Kershaw speculated that Goebbels' deformed right foot played a causal role in his having 'lasting feelings of inadequacy'.

There is an idea with a venerable tradition that there is a correlation between a person's good looks and his or her positive personality traits. It goes back at least to Sappho in the sixth century BC ('What is beautiful is good and who is good will soon also be beautiful'). Perhaps this is just a mistake: 'How complete is the delusion that beauty is goodness', as Tolstoy warned in his *Kreutzer Sonata*. Well, it very likely would be a mistake to think that there is a *direct* causal link between being good-looking and having positive personality traits. But there might be at least one *indirect* causal link from the good looks to the trait – a link that goes via people's conceptions.

Let's assume something for the sake of discussion (it may well be true as far as I know). Let's assume that we mistakenly take there to be a *direct* causal link between having wide-apart eyes and having a friendly, outgoing, non-predatory personality. (Perhaps we assume this link because predatory animals such as wolves tend to have eyes that are closer together than non-predatory animals such as deer.) Mary's eyes are more wide-apart than Jane's. So, because we assume the direct link, we tend to treat Mary as more friendly and outgoing than Jane. Then, if Mary is treated that way (for no *good* reason), she may well come to see herself as more friendly and outgoing than Jane. And, seeing herself that way, she may start to behave in a friendly and outgoing manner, whilst Jane, coming to see herself as more introverted, behaves accordingly.

This example brings out a very interesting point about human psychology, which marks us off from other sentient creatures, and which I'll return to in Chapter 3. We are *self-reflective creatures*. We're capable not only of having a perspective on the world, as a wolf or a deer does. We're also capable of being aware of our own perspective and that of others: to have all the complexity of thought that goes with *reflective consciousness*, where that term covers both self-consciousness and other-consciousness. Thus, it is Mary's thinking that *others* think that she is friendly and outgoing, and that they like her for it, that leads to her coming to think of herself that she's friendly and outgoing, and to behave that way.

Astrology provides a wonderful example of how a trait can in this way develop for anomalous reasons, and yet still become embedded as a fixed part of the personality. According to astrology, people's personality traits tend to correlate with the star sign under which they were born. I, for example, am a Scorpio, and Scorpios are said to be committed, loyal, imaginative, discerning, subtle, persistent and determined (on the good side), and overemotional, hypersensitive, moody, devious, changeable, self-pitying, jealous, unforgiving, unstable, gullible and untidy (on the bad side).

Now this direct correlation is surely false (how could my date of birth have a direct causal influence on my personality?), and we would be crazy to believe it. But many people do believe it; many people are gullible.[9] And their believing it can have an effect on how their personality traits turn out: amongst those who do believe in astrology, their personality traits do indeed tend to cluster around whatever is the paradigm for their particular star sign. If I believed in astrology, I might be overemotional, hypersensitive and jealous because of that (and not for some other reason).

This is a fascinating phenomenon. It is intimately related to the whole business of stereotyping people, which is the topic of Chapter 3. But we can already see how self-fulfilling stereotyping can be. Our thinking that there is a correlation between Mary's good looks and her being friendly and outgoing leads her to act out the trait that is allotted to her; then things really do start to go better for her.[10]

SEEING THE FRIENDLINESS IN THE FACE

So far in this chapter I've been mainly concerned with what a personality trait is, its importance in our everyday discourse, and the relation between personality traits and other attributes of the person. I now turn to an epistemological question, one to do with knowledge and belief. How do we know or come to believe that someone has a particular trait?

One might think that all our knowledge of people's personality traits (where it is genuine knowledge and not error) must be arrived at by inference. For surely psychological dispositions aren't at all the kind of thing one can perceive, as others' minds are necessarily hidden from view. All knowledge about such things must surely be by inference from what one perceives – bodily movements, facial configurations, and so on.

I think this is wrong. To start with, let's consider whether knowledge of someone else's *occurrent* thoughts and feelings has to be arrived at by inference, and then turn to dispositional states of mind – to personality traits.

My claim is that one can *see* friendliness in an action or in a facial expression; the knowledge that this person is being friendly is perceptual, and not inferential. Why should someone reject this? Well, there are, at least, three thoughts that motivate its rejection, and the insistence on the opposing claim, that the best that one can do is *infer* the friendliness, and that all this talk of *seeing* and of perceptual knowledge is just metaphorical or figurative.

The first thought is that one could be wrong. One could think one sees friendliness in the other person's face, but really it's just a very good piece of acting by the other person. So one can't see the friendliness.

We can accept that we can be wrong in such cases. If we were wrong, then of course we wouldn't have seen the friendliness; it would only seem to us as if we had. But it doesn't follow from this that, when we're right, all we see are the mere bodily movements, the mere contours of the face, and the rest is inference: we make either a correct inference, or, if he is acting, an incorrect one. The right thing to say is this: either we see the friendliness, or it merely seems to us as if we do.

A second thought that motivates the opposing view is that if we were asked why we think someone is having friendly thoughts and feelings, we might reply 'Because of the way she looked', thus revealing the inference, from the way she looked to the belief about the thoughts and feelings.

But this appeal to evidence needn't be taken to show that our thought that she was having friendly thoughts and feelings was covertly arrived at by inference. The appeal to evidence shows, rather, that we didn't arrive at the belief out of the blue; we believe she's friendly because she looks that way – friendly. It doesn't show that there was an inference. Consider a different example. You see that the bar on the electric fire is hot. You're asked why you think it's hot, and you reply 'Because of the way it looks.' But need there have been an inference from your seeing the way it looks (glowing red) to your believing it to be hot, or can you just see that it's hot (it looks hot)?

A third thought motivating the view that our beliefs about people's occurrent thoughts and feelings must be inferential is this: if two of us see the same things (behaviour, facial contours, etc.) and one of us comes to believe that the third person is having friendly thoughts and feelings, whilst the other doesn't, then it must follow that this belief is arrived at inferentially, one of us making the inference and the other not.

But this is question-begging. The reply is just to deny that in these circumstances the two of us do see the same thing. The two of us could be looking in the same direction, at the same person, but *see* different things: one sees the friendliness, and the other doesn't. Analogously, the parent could see that the electric fire is hot, whilst the child just sees that the bars are red and doesn't see that the fire is hot. Or – a different example – the expert psychologist could see that his patient is depressed (he looks depressed), whilst his intern doesn't see it.

And this last example now leads directly to the even more controversial claim: not only can one gain non-inferential knowledge, through perception, of another person's occurrent thoughts and feelings; one can also gain non-inferential knowledge, through perception, of someone's personality, of their dispositional state of mind. Here is Lytton Strachey on Florence Nightingale: 'As she passed through the wards in her plain dress, so quiet, so unassuming, she struck the casual observer simply as the pattern of a perfect lady; but the keener eye perceived something more than that – the serenity of high deliberation in the scope of the capacious brow, the sign of power in the dominating curve of the thin nose, and the traces of a harsh and dangerous temper – something peevish, something mocking, and yet something precise – in the small and delicate mouth.'[11]

Although I can't see how to *prove* that my view is right, the view that I am arguing for here – that we can *see* the friendliness in the face, the peevish temper in the small and delicate mouth – is not refuted by any of the three thoughts that I've discussed. And the possibility that my view is right is important.[12] It's important in this context because it is opposed to what I think is a popular misconception: that everything mental, especially everything in the minds of other people, is essentially hidden from view. And it is important also in another context, in Chapter 2, where I will discuss how having a character trait can involve having a perceptual capacity, a sort of expertise, that others lack: for example, the kind person will be able to *see* that someone needs help, whereas the thoughtless person will not, even though they are both looking in the same direction, at the same person who needs help.

WHERE WE'VE GOT TO AND WHERE WE'RE GOING

Let me try to summarise where we've got to so far. Discourse about personality is everywhere. And it's everywhere largely because it's so useful, enabling us to describe, judge, understand, explain and predict. Personality traits, which are very diverse in kind, are, roughly, relatively enduring dispositions. Character traits are reason-responsive dispositions. Discourse about people's personality traits is intermingled with talk of their other attributes – their jobs, their physical appearance, and so on. And these other attributes are connected to personality traits in diverse ways. These connections sometimes enable us to *see* that someone has some trait or other.

The next chapter is mainly about character – about virtue and vice – and about the depth of character traits, as contrasted with personality traits. What will emerge over the chapters to come will be just how fragile and idealised our notion of character is.

Two

CHARACTER: AN OUT-OF-DATE IDEA?

The broad idea of personality that I've been putting forward is one that includes not only personality traits but also character traits. So far I've said that character traits are, in some sense, deeper than personality traits, and that character traits are concerned with a person's moral worth. I now want to say what I mean by this and to show that character (virtue and vice) is important in our thinking about people in ways that might not be immediately apparent.

But there's a difficulty that I must deal with before I begin. There is a view that one hears expressed quite often these days, that character is an out-of-date idea, and has been *replaced* by the modern idea of personality. Character, people say, is a Victorian idea, rightly abandoned along with the British Empire, chastity, pomade, cloth coverings to the legs of a piano, and what Wilfred Owen called the old Lie – that terrible line from Horace, *dulce et decorum est pro patria mori*. Why should people think this?

The Victorian idea of character, I think, is particularly associated with two other ideas, also thought to be out of date: the idea of duty, as fixed by one's allotted 'station' in life; and the idea of self-control and discipline. Your 'station', supposedly, is settled by your role in society, and there is little or nothing that you can do about it. Victorian novels are full of parvenus who aspire to great wealth, but even if they achieve the wealth that they aspire to, as did Melmotte in Trollope's *The Way We Live Now*, they are still seen through; and they usually get their comeuppance.

In Kazuo Ishiguro's *The Remains of the Day*, Stevens is a butler, a son of a butler, and very much of the old school. In the novel, Stevens, as narrator, sets out his concept of what he calls 'dignity', which, to his mind, is the essential quality of a good butler:

'dignity' has to do crucially with a butler's ability not to abandon the professional being he inhabits. Lesser butlers will abandon their professional being for the private one at the least provocation. For such persons, being a butler is like playing some pantomime role; a small push, a slight stumble, and the façade will drop off to reveal the actor underneath. The great butlers are great by virtue of their ability to inhabit their professional role and inhabit it to the utmost; they will not be shaken by external events, however surprising, alarming or vexing.

This passage captures very well the idea of character that we now consider to be out of date: duty and station; self-control and discipline. And, as the novel progresses, we see Stevens living out his professional being, with iron self-control, in the end to tragic effect.

Of course one might agree that this idea of character is out of date, but mourn its passing, rather than celebrate it. The contemporary philosopher Anthony Quinton has said that it's regrettable that character, embodied as it was in the Victorian way of life, is no longer to be found today. In what he admits is a somewhat 'legislative' way, Quinton identifies character not so much with role as with self-control or strength of will – as 'the disposition or habit of controlling one's immediate, impulsive desires so that we do not let them issue in action until we have considered the bearing of that action on the achievement of other, remoter, objects of desire'. These days, Quinton mourns, everyday morality consists of two styles: 'negatively permissive' and 'ecstatic'. We should, he thinks, 'reinstate character in life and in education'.[1]

I think it's true that the ideal of character as strength of will, toughness, resistance to temptation, self-control, often allied to the idea of duty and station, was peculiarly Victorian (as were the public schools designed to develop these things in the well-bred). But the identification of character with these notions is a mistake, as we'll see in Chapter 3. What Quinton is doing is defining character as the Victorians did (or as some Victorians did), and then saying that character, *thus defined*, is defunct.

FROM THE SPECIFIC TO THE GENERAL

We shouldn't confuse these two thoughts: the thought that the idea of character is out of date; and the thought that the Victorian idea of character is out of date. Obviously the latter thought could be true and the former false. And this is just how things are. Aristotle is important here, not just philosophically, but also historically.

Aristotle, especially in his *Nicomachean Ethics*, gave an account of what it is to be a man of virtuous character. In the broad strokes of its analysis, it remains unparalleled in its insights, and the outline is as much with us today as it was in his day, and as it was before his day, for the notion of character wasn't made up by him. But in its specifics, Aristotle's analysis aimed to give an account of what sort of qualities of character are desirable in an aristocratic man (yes, specifically a man), living in a small fifth-century BC city state – Athens. Such a man would be great-minded or great-souled. He would have no humility, as it is appropriate for him to be proud of having a good moral character, and to think himself worthy of great things. He would have character traits that only someone with his kind of breeding and upbringing could have; for example, he would have the virtues of not abusing his power and of munificence, and these are traits of character that automatically exclude not only slaves, but also other people who, by the contingency of birth perhaps, lack power and wealth, such as ordinary tradesmen – as well as all women.

My contention, now, is that we need not be committed to this idea of character in all its specificity. What we want is a more general notion of character, one that can be applied to all human beings, whether English or Greek, whether contemporary or historical, whether rich or poor, whether butler or aristocrat, whether man or woman, whether well brought up or badly brought up. It is this general notion that I will be trying to capture. And, in doing this, I will be drawing a lot on Aristotle: looking for what is general to all social human beings underneath what is specifically fifth-century BC Athenian.

But, by the way, for those who are interested in the specificity of Athenian ideas of character and personality, I recommend a book by a pupil of Aristotle's: Theophrastus' *Characters*. Each of thirty character and personality traits is defined, and there then follows for each trait a list of what that kind of person does. Here is what Theophrastus says about obnoxiousness:

> It is not difficult to define obnoxiousness: it is joking that is obvious and offensive. The obnoxious man is the sort who,

when he meets respectable women, raises his cloak and exposes his genitals. In the theatre he claps after others have stopped, and hisses the actors when the others enjoy watching. When the audience is silent he rears back and belches, to make the spectators turn around. When the agora is crowded he goes to the stands for walnuts, myrtleberries, and fruits, and stands there nibbling on them while talking with the vendor. He calls out by name to someone in the crowd with whom he's not acquainted. When he sees people hurrying somewhere he tells them to wait. He goes up to a man who has lost an important case and is leaving the court, and congratulates him. He goes shopping for himself and hires flute girls, and he shows his purchases to anyone he meets and invites them to share. He stands by the barber shop or perfume seller and relates that he intends to get drunk.[2]

CHARACTER: DEPTH AND MORALITY

What do I mean when I say that character traits are deeper than personality traits, and that they are concerned with a person's moral worth?

There was a story told by the British Labour Party politician Denis Healey, which illustrates the idea of character being deep. The story was about David Owen, another Labour politician, who fell out with his colleagues for all sorts of reasons that I don't need to go into. Healey's story was this: 'Four fairies attended the birth of David Owen. Number One said "You'll be good-looking." Number Two said "You'll be very clever." Number Three said "You'll be very ambitious." Number Four said "You'll be all these things, and you'll also be a shit." '

This is a funny story, and one that was meant to wound.

Whether or not there is truth in it is irrelevant here, for I want to use it to develop the idea of character and depth. The fourth fairy had fixed a *character trait* of Owen's, and this character trait affects or colours our judgement of Owen's other attributes, determined by the first three fairies. Our response to the story is to feel that his good looks, his cleverness, his ambition, are, so to speak, polluted by his character trait of being a shit. Traits that would otherwise have been good have been neutralised or even made bad by a bad character trait. In contrast, if the fourth fairy had just added a bad personality trait (being highly strung, being extraordinarily shy), the rest of his personality would be unpolluted by this bad trait.

Thus, someone's personality traits are only good conditionally upon that person also having good character traits. Immanuel Kant made a similar kind of point when talking about a scoundrel's coolness, coolness being a personality trait (a talent or skill): 'the very coolness of a scoundrel makes him, not merely more dangerous, but also immediately more abominable in our eyes than we should have taken him to be without it'.[3]

On the other hand, the converse isn't true: the goodness of someone's character traits is not good conditionally on his having good personality traits. Someone is a wise, honest and kind person; but he has absolutely no sense of humour. Whilst your being told about this man's lack of a sense of humour might lead you to choose not to spend an evening in the pub with him, this bad personality trait doesn't pollute his wisdom, his honesty, his kindness or his other good character traits. This is an example of what I mean when I say that character traits have more depth than personality traits.

The other thing that the Healey story reveals is that

character traits, such as being a shit, are concerned with a person's *moral* worth. We judge Owen morally for being a shit in a way that we wouldn't if he were highly strung or shy. Also – and it is highly controversial whether or not we are right to do this – we hold him morally responsible for having this trait. This is the topic of Chapter 4.

Even if all the talk these days, in the Press, on TV, is centred on personality, surface, appearance, charisma and just on 'being a personality', and little on virtue and vice, deep down we still make this distinction between character and personality, and attach great moral weight to character.

To begin to show this, I want now to consider action, motive and character and the relation between them. Some philosophers think that the assessment of a moral action, and of its consequences, can and should be made regardless of motive and character. Others, rightly in my view, think that motive and character are all-important. We need to consider this in more detail to see why and how motive and character matter.

MY BROKEN-DOWN CAR: MILL AND HUME

One evening I was driving through the pouring rain in the London rush-hour traffic, when suddenly my car stalled in the middle of the road. All the electrics were dead. I immediately saw the only thing I could do was to try to push the car to the side of the road, and then call the rescue services on my mobile. But the car was a heavy automatic and wouldn't budge. So I was stuck, holding up all the traffic, and causing irritation all round. Car after car passed me and I saw the drivers looking at me angrily. Then someone – I didn't find out his name – stopped, got out of his car, and cheerfully helped me push my car to the roadside. He was wearing a dinner jacket and it got completely soaked and muddy in the process. Finally, with a friendly wave he got back into his car and drove off.

I was glad to be helped. It got me out of a tricky situation. But here we are concerned with the impact of motive and character on our assessment of this person's action – let's call him Byron. The question is whether I would think the same of Byron's action whatever his motive and whatever his character.

J. S. Mill thought that indeed we do judge the moral rightness of an action – Byron's in this case – regardless of factors concerning motive and character. Drawing a sharp distinction between moral judgements of the action and moral judgements of the person who performs the action, he said:

> the motive has nothing to do with the morality of the action, though much with the worth of the agent. He who saves a man from drowning does what is morally right, whether his motive be duty, or the hope of being paid for his trouble . . . no known ethical standard decides an action to be good or bad because it is done by a good or bad man, still less because done by an amiable, a brave, or a benevolent man, on the contrary. These considerations are relevant, not to the estimation of actions, but of persons.[4]

We might ask ourselves whether Mill is right here – whether this accords with our own 'ethical standards'. But before answering this question, let's look at David Hume, whose views about the relevance of motive and character in the assessment of action are at an opposite extreme to those of Mill. He thought them to be centrally important:

> If any action be either virtuous or vicious, it is only as a sign of some quality or character. It must depend upon durable

principles of the mind, which extend over the whole conduct, and enter into the personal character. Actions themselves, not proceeding from any constant principle, have no influence on love or hatred, pride or humility, and consequently are never considered in morality.[5]

To my mind, both Hume's and Mill's positions seem more extreme – in opposing directions – than our ordinary morality would suggest. Hume's position would imply that I ought to consider Byron's action of helping me not to deserve *any* praise in itself, but only as a 'sign' of his good character – about which, so far as my story goes, we know nothing. So, according to Hume, I ought really to reserve judgement. And Mill's position, on the other hand, would imply that I should consider Byron's action in itself to be deserving of the same degree of gratitude and praise *whatever* the motive, whether selfish or otherwise, and whether done out of a relatively enduring disposition or not.

MY BROKEN-DOWN CAR (CONTINUED): ARISTOTLE AND KANT

Let's now turn to Aristotle's position, which is, I think, closer to our ordinary way of thinking about action, motive and character. Aristotle began his account of virtue and of virtuous action in the *Nicomachean Ethics* by pointing out a disanalogy with the production of a good piece of craftwork, such as a good chair. The disanalogy is this: if someone produces a good chair, we consider the chair to be a good one irrespective of facts about the maker of the chair. Say the maker was a raw apprentice and, just by sheer luck, the first chair he made was an excellently crafted one, then we would say that the chair is just as good as if it had been made by a master craftsman. As Aristotle puts it, it doesn't matter what 'state' the maker of the chair is in, just so long as the chair itself is in 'the right state'.

This is in contrast to our moral judgement of action, Aristotle says, where it is not sufficient that the action itself be in 'the right state' (for example, being an action of saving someone from drowning or an action of helping someone whose car had broken down). The person doing the action, Aristotle says, must be 'in the right state' also. And he then went on to lay down these four conditions that must be met by the person doing the action for it to count as properly a virtuous action: first, the person doing virtuous actions 'must know [that he is doing virtuous actions]; second, he must decide on them, and decide on them for themselves; and, third, he must also do them from a firm and unchanging state'; and fourthly, he must have the right feelings.[6]

We can now apply these four conditions to Byron's action. I think they fit our intuitions very well. First, we would think less of Byron's action if he didn't really know what he was doing, if he did what he did as a result of some sort of mistake. Say, for example, Byron thought mistakenly that the car I was driving contained the consignment of smuggled drugs that was supposed to be delivered to him later that evening, so it was essential for him to get the car out of harm's way; if he had known that it was me, a mere stranger, then he wouldn't even have thought of stopping. It is important in our assessment of the virtuousness or moral goodness of Byron's action that he should know what he was doing.

Secondly, we would think less of Byron's action if his motive wasn't a morally good one – if instead he had an ulterior motive lurking behind his apparent kindness or thoughtfulness. Say he had helped me in order to impress his girlfriend who was with him in his car – perhaps she had just been saying to him how much she admired people who were kind and helpful, and it was only because of this that Byron did what he did. Otherwise he would have passed on by.[7]

Thirdly, our opinion of Byron's action would be affected by whether or not he was doing it out of a relatively enduring disposition (out of a 'firm and unchanging state'). Say his motive was genuinely kind and thoughtful, but it was only because he had just passed his exams that he found himself having such unusually kind thoughts that evening; normally he would not have been moved at all by my plight. Whereas, if what he did was in character or typical of the man, we would think better of the action.

And, fourthly and finally, what sort of feelings and emotions Byron had when he helped me affects what we think of him. Say he knew just what he was doing (the first point), his motive was genuinely kind and thoughtful (the second point), and his action was in character and not done for some unusual reason (the third point), and yet he helped me begrudgingly, and with a bad grace. We would think less of his action if he didn't do what he did willingly, and in a cheerful manner (as, in fact, he did – my story is a true one).

Thus, according to Aristotle, whilst a chair can truly be called excellent regardless of the 'state' of the maker of the chair, our assessment of Byron's action as excellent or virtuous is influenced not only by the action itself and its consequences, but also by these four conditions that Aristotle specified: that he knew what he was doing; that his motive was characteristic of the virtue rather than self-regarding; that he acted out of a relatively enduring disposition; and that he had the right feelings.

There is a fourth great moral philosopher who hasn't been mentioned so far, except in passing, and that is the austere figure of Immanuel Kant. Kant's position is that the only thing that matters in determining whether or not an action is moral is whether or not it is done out of a sense of one's moral duty; just so long as one's motive is 'pure', the action will have moral worth. And this will be so regardless of the consequences of the action – 'let the consequences be what they may'.[8]

But Kant has a very unappealing idea of what a 'pure' motive is. Duty, and duty *alone*, must be the motive. Even if your motive, your reason for doing the action, were one of benevolence (and not one of self-interest), your action would still not count as having moral worth. Aristotle, as we have seen, distinguished a motive characteristic of the virtue – a motive characteristic of kindness for example – from a more self-regarding motive, and for him the former is essential to virtuous action, as is having the right feelings. But for Kant the motive of kindness is mere 'inclination', no better than a self-regarding one in this respect, and the person's feelings when doing the action are irrelevant to its moral worth. In his *Groundwork* there is this famous, or rather infamous, passage, in which Kant gives expression to this extraordinarily counter-intuitive position, and which has given so much trouble to Kantian scholars ever since:

> To help others where one can is a duty, and besides this there are many spirits of so sympathetic a temper that, without any further motive of vanity or self-interest, they find an inner pleasure in spreading happiness around them and can take delight in the contentment of others as their own work. Yet I maintain that in such a case an action of this kind, however right and however amiable it may be, has still no genuine moral worth . . . Suppose then that the mind of this friend of man were overclouded by sorrows of his own which

extinguished all sympathy with the fate of others because sufficiently occupied with his own; and suppose that, when no longer moved by any inclination, he tears himself out of this deadly insensibility and does the action without any inclination for the sake of duty alone; then for the first time his action has its genuine moral worth . . . It is precisely in this that the worth of character begins to show – a moral worth and beyond all comparison the highest – namely, that he does good, not from inclination, but from duty.[9]

This passage (and others like it in the Kantian corpus) led a contemporary of Kant's, Friedrich Schiller, to make a very neat parody of Kant's position with an imagined dialogue:

'Gladly I serve my friends, but alas I also do it with pleasure. Hence I am plagued with doubt that I am not a virtuous person.'

'Sure, your only resource is to try to despise them entirely, and then with aversion to do what your duty enjoins you.'[10]

Recently, philosophers in the Kantian tradition have sought to make Kant's position more amenable to our intuitions and closer to that of Aristotle. (And I agree with them that Kant has something of a response to Schiller's joke.) But still, in my view, their struggle is an uphill one – as evidenced by the nicely chosen title of one recent book in this tradition, by Marcia Baron: *Kantian Ethics Almost Without Apology*.[11]

It should be clear, even from this very brief outline, that there are deep and important differences between these four great moral philosophers over the place of motive and of character in our moral assessment of action. I leave you to consider for yourself which most nearly conforms to your own intuitions. But regardless of this question, all four hold, in their different ways, that motive and character are also *distinct* objects of moral assessment. So now I want to ask why we value virtues or good character traits.

Please remember in what follows that whilst we don't these days use the *words* 'virtue' and 'vice' ('vice' these days has an entirely different sense – 'vice-rings' and so on), we are still talking *about* virtue and vice when we talk about character traits as being good or bad – about Byron's being kind and about David Owen's (supposedly) being a shit. So whilst the *language* that moral philosophers use may be somewhat out of date, the topic is not. There are still kind and generous people, and cruel and heartless ones.

WHAT IS A VIRTUE?

A mere list of virtues (of good character traits) isn't going to tell us what virtue is. Socrates pointed this out long ago. And anyway, people's lists differ. Aristotle, who divided virtues into virtues of character and intellectual virtues, included on his list temperance, courage, justice and, centrally, what is usually translated as practical wisdom, as well as those that I have already mentioned, such as generosity. The paradigmatic Christian virtues included the four 'cardinal virtues' of Aristotle, but also faith, hope, and charity or Christian love (*caritas*). Hume, whose list of virtues included benevolence, pity, and love of children, made a mockery of what he called the 'whole train of monkish virtues', such as celibacy, fasting, penance, mortification, humility, silence and solitude, placing them instead in 'the category of vices'.[12] Nietzsche, an atheist like Hume, also utterly rejected the Christian ascetic virtues, as well as pity and compassion. He put in the place of the traditional Christian virtues the human excellence that would maximise artistic and creative values; 'So that precisely [traditional] morality would be to blame if the *highest power and splendour* actually possible to the type man was never in fact attained? So that precisely [traditional] morality was the danger of dangers?'[13] Not all of these views can be right.

How then to make progress? One might try saying that what makes a trait a virtue is its being a trait that we approve of. For example, kindness is a virtue because we approve of this trait in people: we are proud of it in ourselves and we admire it in others. But this can't be right because it is quite possible that there are traits that we approve of but that aren't *really* virtues – that is, they are not *really* good traits. For example, ruthlessness might be thought well of in a hard, militaristic society, or greed on Gordon Gekko's Wall Street ('Greed is good'), but they aren't really virtues. And one of Nietzsche's central thoughts about our conventional morality was just like that: what 'we' approve of as virtues (compassion, pity, humility and so on) are really no such thing.

So we might instead try saying that a virtue is a trait that *ought* to be approved of, or that is approved of by right-thinking people. This has the merit of being true, but it is singularly unhelpful. For the following question is then pressing: *Why* do right-thinking people approve of it? And the answer, on pain of circularity, should not be that they approve of it because it is a virtue.[14] What we need to do is to find a grounding for what we approve of or value – in this case virtue. And this grounding should reveal reasons, which are reasons *both* why a particular trait is a virtue, *and* why right-thinking people approve of it. The question then turns into where to look for this grounding. Let's look at what Hume and Aristotle say.

A GROUNDING FOR VIRTUE

Hume looked for a grounding for the virtues (for good character traits) in their 'being useful or agreeable to the person himself or to others'.[15] Courage and temperance, discretion, industry, sense and wisdom (all examples of Hume's) are useful to the person himself. Benevolence and love of children benefit those nearest and dearest to us. Honesty, fidelity and truthfulness tend to promote the interests of a wider society. And the 'monkish virtues' are really vices, because, Hume said, 'they serve no manner of purpose; neither advance a man's fortune in the world, nor render him a more valuable member of society; neither qualify him for the entertainment of company, nor increase his power of self-enjoyment'.[16]

Aristotle's approach was to look for the grounding of the virtues in human nature – in an account of what it is to be a flourishing human being. According to him, a virtue is a trait (a 'firm and unchanging state') that enables a human being to live his life well as a human being, which is as a social and political animal.[17]

At this stage – and I hope this isn't disappointing – I am not going to argue in favour of a particular set of character traits as virtues and vices, nor am I going to provide a critical evaluation of Hume's or Aristotle's account (or Nietzsche's, or anyone else's in particular) of how the virtues should be grounded. The point of the foregoing discussion, rather, is to indicate the essential dependence of an account of what traits we take to be virtues and vices on our wider views about what is valuable in the world. We value traits, calling them virtues, because they are dispositions reliably to recognise what is of value or disvalue in the world, and reliably to respond appropriately in thought, feeling and action. Intellectual virtues, such as wisdom, and moral virtues, such as benevolence and being just, have precisely this feature. We value wisdom because we value truth. We value benevolence because we value such things as security and comfort, and we disvalue cruelty because we disvalue such things as pain and needless suffering. And so on for justice and the other virtues. What you value in the world will determine what character traits you value in yourself and in others.

Another way of putting what is at the heart of virtue is that *a virtue is a trait that is reliably responsive to good reasons, to reasons that reveal values; it is reason-responsive in the right way*. I had better explain what I mean in some detail, as it will be of great importance in the rest of this chapter, and in chapters 3 and 4. I'll put it briefly to begin with, in a way that mightn't be immediately intelligible. Then I'll use a little story to illustrate what I mean. And then I'll return to the question of value and to the idea of a moral upbringing or attunement into a world of value.

VIRTUE AND REASON: TRISHA'S FRIENDS

Character traits, I said in Chapter 1, are reason-responsive: dispositions reliably to respond to certain kinds of reasons. Virtues – kindness, for example – are responsive to *good* reasons. Someone with a virtue can be relied on to be aware of the evaluative significance of his or her circumstances and surroundings, and to think, feel and act as he or she should. Vices – cruelty, for example – are responsive to bad reasons. And if someone lacks a virtue, without having the corresponding vice, then he or she isn't responsive to good reasons.

Now for the story. It's Trisha's thirtieth birthday, and she and four guests, Susan, Charles, Ian and Lucy, are having dinner together in a restaurant. Trisha is being teased by the others about being thirty (over the hill, past her best, still not married, and so on). To start with, she doesn't really mind because she likes being the centre of attention. But by the time the main course arrives, she is beginning to get upset, and is close to tears. The teasing is getting to her. Here, then, we have a fact: *that Trisha is getting upset and is close to tears*. Facts can be reasons for one thing and not for another. And this particular fact is a reason – that is, a *good* reason – for her four guests to stop teasing her. This is what we mean when we say that they should stop teasing her *because* she is getting upset and is close to tears; the 'because' here points to a reason. If you ask me why the fact that Trisha is getting upset and is close to tears is a reason to stop teasing her, I would reply that being upset in these circumstances is a bad thing because it involves needless tears and suffering, and one ought to do what one can to avoid causing needless tears and suffering. If you then asked me why needless tears and suffering are a bad thing, I suppose I could continue, but I would suspect that you are not being serious (or perhaps you are a philosopher trying to make the point that my explanation doesn't go deep enough).

Anyway, what happens next in my little story is that Trisha's four friends have different motives and act in different ways – differences that reveal, and are expressive of, their different characters.

Susan quickly becomes aware that Trisha is going to cry, and, with characteristic sensitivity, sees what ought to be done, and does it. She is kind, but she is not only kind: she is also sufficiently sensitive to appreciate that the right thing to do is not to put her arm around Trisha and apologise for the teasing. The right thing to do is just discreetly to change the subject. How does Susan know what the right thing to do is? Is there some general rule that she is applying to this particular case? No, her kindness, her sensitivity and her practical wisdom (her common sense) just enable her to appreciate what should be done in this particular case. As Aristotle puts it, the virtuous person (like Susan here) will feel and act 'at the right times, about the right things, towards the right people, and in the right way . . . this is the intermediate and best condition, and this is proper to virtue'.[18] Susan, true to her kindness, is thus showing her awareness of the evaluative significance of her circumstances, and is thinking, feeling and acting as she should – as the circumstances require. And we value her kindness, and her kind action, because of its role in helping avoid needless tears and suffering, and we *disvalue* needless tears and suffering (don't ask me why – we've been over that already).

The idea that Susan can see what is the right thing to do here should remind you of the discussion in Chapter 1 of how someone with the right sensitivity can see the friendliness in a face, or in a gesture, where others might miss it. Here we have a comparable idea: someone with the right sensitivity – the kind person – can see what the right thing to do is, where others – those who are not kind – might not. John McDowell, a contemporary philosopher who has been very influential in these matters, puts it like this: 'A kind person has a reliable sensitivity to a certain sort of requirement that situations impose on behaviour . . . The sensitivity is, we might say, a sort of perceptual capacity.'[19]

The second guest at the dinner, Charles, is not a nice person at all. Like Susan, he quickly sees that Trisha is getting upset and is close to tears. But he sees this fact not as a reason to change the subject, but as a reason to keep on at her until she bursts into tears. And this is what he does. He wants to have some fun at her expense. Charles, then, is acting on a reason – a reason in the psychological sense – but this reason is not a good one. The fact that she's getting upset may explain why he's carrying on pushing her to tears but, I hope we all agree, it's a *lousy* reason to do so. It's a good reason to stop and it's a bad reason to carry on. Charles is being responsive to bad reasons because he's a swine, a shit. Not much of a friend, and we think badly of him – of his character, of his motives and of his action.

It's not as though Charles is failing to pick up on how Trisha is feeling. He sees that she's getting upset just as clearly as Susan does. This example shows, then, that we shouldn't always assume that the swines, the intentionally nasty people in the world, are necessarily *unaware* of people's suffering; in fact it's often the sensitively aware torturer, jailer, sadist, who is more effective in carrying out his or her purposes – more effective, that is, than the insensitive thug.

The third guest, Ian, doesn't notice that Trisha is getting upset and is close to tears. This fact, as we have seen, is a reason – a good reason – to stop teasing her. But because Ian doesn't notice this fact, he carries on with his teasing. It's not as though Ian is positively unpleasant. It's just that he's inconsiderate: he lacks the virtue of kindness and consideration for others. Lacking this virtue, he doesn't spot that Trisha is getting upset. To use Kant's very neat way of putting the point, Ian is neither +A (having the virtue), nor –A (having the vice), but 0 (zero, lacking the virtue).[20]

Trisha's fourth guest, Lucy, sees that Trisha is getting upset and is close to tears, and, at first, appreciates that this is a reason to stop teasing her. But Charles whispers in her ear a whole lot of psychobabble to the effect that Trisha has a deep unconscious longing to be teased and brought to tears, and generally to have her inferiority emphasised in front of all her friends. Lucy believes all this, and thus comes to believe that what Charles has told her is a reason to carry on with the teasing. She has an intellectual vice, gullibility, being a disposition to believe what she is told on vastly inadequate evidence. By the way, Lucy nicely illustrates the point that intellectual vices, such as gullibility, are not just harmful to the possessor of the vice: they can lead to harm to others too. And the converse also applies to the intellectual virtues: they can be useful and helpful to others.

This little story of virtue and vice, of good and bad character traits, will, I hope, go some way to showing what a virtue is, what virtuous motives are, and why we value virtue and disvalue vice. Of course we also value charm, good looks, skill at dancing, and an ability to play winning cross-court backhands. Later, not until Chapter 4, will we see why, and in what respects, virtues – moral and intellectual – differ from skills, talents and other aspects of personality in this respect: we can be morally responsible for our virtues and vices in quite different ways from our responsibility for our skills and talents.

ATTUNEMENT INTO A WORLD OF VALUE

How do we come to be virtuous (if we do)? We are born, as social animals, into a cultural world of value and disvalue – a world where certain things *matter*, as harmful, dangerous, comforting, warming and so on. If we have been brought up in the right way, we will be disposed reliably to recognise these values and disvalues and to respond as we should: as Aristotle says, 'at the right times, about the right things, towards the right people, and in the right way'. And if this happens, then we will care in the right way about the things that matter: not simply caring for justice and kindness as if for some vague idea, but caring that *particular* people in *particular* circumstances are treated as they should be – with fairness, honesty and consideration, so that we get angry (justifiably angry) if this doesn't happen. It will become 'second nature' to have these responses, so that our own interests, narrowly conceived, are quite naturally far from being our only consideration in deciding what to do. Being disposed reliably to be motivated by specifically other-regarding moral considerations is part of what it is to have a virtue.

But a problem arises here which I like to call the Equity Union problem, named after a story that used to be (and perhaps still is) told by out-of-work aspiring actors. The aspiring actor says to the theatre producer that he wants to act in some play or other. The producer replies that he can do so only if he is a member of Equity, the actors' union. Does he have an Equity card? 'No, I haven't', says the actor, 'how do I get one?' 'Well, you have to be acting first.' To get a union card you need to act. To act you need a union card. That's the Equity Union problem. It's structurally similar, roughly, to Joseph Heller's Catch-22; like Yossarian, you should whistle in admiration.

The analogous problem here is that to become virtuous, you must do virtuous actions, acting out of virtuous motives. And to do virtuous actions out of virtuous motives, you must first be virtuous.

The way out of this problem (I leave to one side the question of how to become a member of Equity) is to appreciate that, to begin with, a child's upbringing into the cultural world of value is indirect in just the following sense. 'Tim, if you look after your little sister whilst I am watering the garden, I'll let you stay up to watch TV'; 'If you don't play fairly with your sister, Tim, then no dinner for you tonight.' These reasons that are being given to Tim as to why he should do what morality requires – be caring, act fairly – are not specifically other-regarding moral reasons. So at this stage Tim isn't really virtuous, even if he does what his mother asks. It is only over time, through habituation, that Tim comes to see that there are distinctly *moral* reasons for him to do these things – to see that it *matters* that he should care for, and play fairly with, his little sister, even without the incentive of the stick or the carrot administered by his mother. And then, coming to appreciate these moral reasons, he comes to act on them – to be motivated by them. The philosopher Myles Burnyeat explains this process in a wonderful discussion of Aristotle's idea of moral education:

> I may be told, and may believe, that such and such actions are just and noble, but I have not really learned for myself (taken to heart, made second nature to me) that they have intrinsic value until I have learned to value (love) them for it, with the consequence that I take pleasure in doing them. To understand and appreciate the value that makes them enjoyable in themselves, I must learn for myself to enjoy them, and that does take time and practice – in short, habituation.[21]

So what happens when we bring up our children to be good is that, to begin with, their actions are, so to speak, simulacra of virtuous actions, because they are done for non-moral reasons and not for moral reasons. Even if Tim realises, perhaps because his mother tells him so, that there *are* moral reasons to care for and be fair to his sister, it is only once he acts *for these reasons* that the action becomes truly a virtuous one. We've all heard children 'mouthing' moral reasons for their being kind or truthful when we know that really they're doing it to please Mummy, or to be well thought of, or to avoid punishment.

Sometimes, even in later life, people do the morally right things not for morally good reasons but for other reasons – remember Mill's example of the drowning man and the reward. We tell the truth because we're afraid that we'll be found out if we lie. The fact that we'll get found out if we lie might be a good reason to tell the truth, but it is not a good *moral* reason. And we've all heard adults 'mouthing' moral reasons when the real source of their motivation isn't any such thing.

WHERE WE'VE GOT TO AND WHERE WE'RE GOING

I hope I have shown in this chapter that the idea of character isn't out of date. It's still with us, and Aristotle captures it very well, once we abstract from the specifics of his account to get to something like a core notion. And we all care about character, and not just about surface, about appearance, about the mask or veneer of mere personality. We want our President or Prime Minister to have a good character; we want to marry, or live with, people who are kind and thoughtful; we want our children to be good, and not just fun to be with. Of course we want the wit, the charm, the *je ne sais quoi* too, but when the chips are down, these are not enough.

There's a difficulty with what I have said so far about character. It may seem as if I am saying that it's very easy reliably to act in the right way, just so long as you have been properly brought up to appreciate the evaluative significance of your circumstances and to see what ought, morally speaking, to be done. In our ordinary thinking about morality, we tend to think of character traits as being robust: stable and consistent in their manifestation in thought, feeling and action across a wide range of different situations – virtuous action smoothly, reliably, follows from a virtuous character; honest people can be relied on to act honestly wherever honesty is appropriate. I'll try to show that this ordinary way of thinking is mistaken about our actual psychology: character is much more fragile than we think. What this reveals is a sort of idealism about character, which leads us to expect of our character traits more than we realistically should. A proper understanding of character traits will help us to correct that tendency, and to be better able to find our way in a world of value that can sometimes test and tempt us, and find us wanting, in surprising ways and in surprising circumstances. And it will be revealing to see that this was anticipated by Aristotle too, in his superb account of weakness of the will.

The Fragility of Character
Three

OUR BAD PRACTICES

In Chapter 1 I said that talk of personality and character is pervasive. But is it *too* pervasive? Are we overly inclined, in our thought and talk about personality and character, to ascribe traits to people, often on the basis of little evidence? I think we are. We are too prone to pigeon-hole people, and I'll begin this chapter by looking at two of our bad practices in this area: stereotyping and prejudice; and what I will call 'give a dog a bad name'.

Experiments in social psychology also lend support to the idea that, in fact, people don't have the traits that we so readily ascribe to them: honesty, kindness, friendliness and so on – stable traits, consistent across a wide range of situations. Character is fragile. But this doesn't mean that we have to abandon all talk of personality and character. We can avoid the mistakes and harm that are amongst the products of our bad practices, whilst not finding ourselves bereft of what is an essential part of our way of thinking of ourselves and others. For we need to think and talk about personality and character traits to explain and to predict people's thoughts, feelings and actions. Moreover, we need to think and talk about character traits – virtues and vices – as part of our moral thought and talk about people. What will emerge here is a kind of idealism about character: where we value a trait in ourselves or in others, we tend to idealise the kinds of motivations that the trait involves. Roughly speaking, in expecting the best of ourselves and of others, we expect more than human beings are really capable of. So, not surprisingly, we're often disappointed: people fail to act according to the ideal.

THE FIRST BAD PRACTICE: STEREOTYPING AND PREJUDICE

The first bad practice involves, roughly, leaping to conclusions about someone's personality on the strength of what we know about his or her nationality, job, place of residence, or some other attribute. This is stereotyping. And it often comes with prejudice: the presupposition that the personality traits of strangers, foreigners and so forth are bad ones. These prejudices are often based on fear.

David Hume discussed these matters in a very nice essay called 'Of National Characters'. He starts his essay with an important distinction, between what the 'vulgar' do (that is, those without the proper education and training), and what 'men of sense' do:

> The vulgar are apt to carry all national characters to extremes, and having once established it as a principle that any people are knavish, or cowardly, or ignorant, they will admit of no exception but comprehend every individual under the same censure. Men of sense condemn these undistinguished judgements, though, at the same time, they allow that each nation has a peculiar set of manners, and that some particular qualities are more frequently to be met with among one people than among their neighbours.[1]

Hume is surely right to condemn what the 'vulgar' do, turning generalisations into exceptionless laws: all X's are

Y – all Spaniards are haughty, all policemen are bullies, all women love babies, all redheads are temperamental. Most of us, I dare say, are guilty of it from time to time; the German press and the Italian press regularly swap stereotypes, as do the French and the English. (The relation here between carica-ture and character is interesting; a caricature or sketch – the etymology of the word is nothing to do with the etymology of 'character' – necessarily exaggerates the way someone looks, and this exaggeration is often tied to a covert or overt suggestion that anyone who looks like *that* is bound to be of a certain exaggerated personality type; think here of some of the caricatures of capitalists used in Marxist propaganda.)

However, Hume insists, it is sensible (what a man of sense will do) to make generalisations about national character-istics, professions and so forth, and to use them to guide our actions, so long as we remember, which the 'man of sense' will do, that it is a generalisation and that it only holds 'gener-ally, and for the most part'.

Of course, one should only use generalisations as a guide if they are good ones, where by 'good' I mean both useful and true for the most part. And the problem with most of these kinds of generalisations is not that they are generalisations, nor that they can't be true, but that they fail to be useful. This is because the variations amongst people within any nation or culture or profession or gender or hair-colour group are so great – greater than the variations between the average or what is 'typical' for any given nation or culture and so on. The average or 'typical' New Yorker may be more sophisticated than the average West Texan, but there are many very unsophisticated New Yorkers, and many highly cultured and urbane West Texans. So the generalisation ('New Yorkers are more sophisticated than West Texans') is going to be of hardly any predictive or explanatory usefulness about any particular person.[2]

THE SECOND BAD PRACTICE: GIVE A DOG A BAD NAME

The second bad practice involves, roughly, leaping to conclusions about someone's personality on the strength of insufficient behavioural evidence.

One evening you go to dinner at a friend's house, and you find yourself sitting next to a fellow guest. You've never met him before. Throughout the dinner, which is generally a jolly affair, he behaves in a very gloomy way, saying little, and what he does say is all very negative and depressing. It is, I think, a natural inclination for us to think that he is a gloomy and morose person. What have we done here? We have inferred from his gloomy and morose behaviour during that one evening that he is *disposed* to be that way. The implication is that he'll be predictably gloomy and morose at dinner parties – call this *stability* of the trait; and, moreover, that he'll be gloomy and morose across a broad and diverse range of situations and not just at dinner parties – call this *consistency* of the trait. From now on, let's call the combination of stability and consistency *robustness*. That is what we mean when we say that he is a gloomy and morose person.

This is lazy. We haven't got enough evidence to say that this person has these robust traits. There could be all sorts of other explanations for his being that way during that particular evening – the real story might be quite different. Perhaps he was only gloomy and morose with you, because he found your line in dinner party conversation particularly boring; with others he is disposed to be great fun. Or perhaps he just happened to be in a gloomy and morose mood that evening because he had had an unusually bad day at work.

Once we have fixed on the theory that this person has these robust traits, we then tend to be subject to another kind of error in reasoning: it's called the *confirmation bias*: 'Given a hypothesis, one tends to look for confirming evidence. Finding such evidence, one takes it to support the hypothesis. Evidence against the hypothesis tends to be ignored or downplayed.'[3] Imagine that you find yourself sitting next to this fellow guest at another dinner party (in spite of your pleas for a revised *placement*). You expect him to be gloomy and morose (stability). If he is, you consider your theory confirmed, even though it might just be because he's sitting next to *you* again. And if, this particular evening, much to your surprise, you find him really rather garrulous and friendly, you don't consider your theory disconfirmed: 'Well', you think to yourself, 'this fellow is acting out of character tonight; I wonder why he's not being his usual self.' The picture is not unfamiliar. The dog has a bad name, and nothing he does will prove otherwise. This, again, is what the vulgar do, and most of us are prone to it from time to time.

Of course, the saying is 'give a dog a bad name . . . and *hang him*'. So this bad practice extends to thinking that, once someone's bad reputation is fixed or settled in our minds, then they must be to blame for all sorts of thing that happen (consistency). If one day you hear that your fellow guest took part in a fun run that turned out to be a miserable affair, you readily conclude that it was he that cast a pall on the whole thing. We might call this the Round Up the Usual Suspects principle, after its application by Chief of Police Louis Renault, the Claude Rains character in *Casablanca*.

I call this practice 'give a dog a bad name', rightly so, because we are prone to what's called a *negativity bias*: we're more likely to attribute a negative personality trait on little evidence than a positive one.[4] But the practice does also extend to giving people a good name on insufficient behavioural evidence. Remember Byron, who helped me move my car to the side of the road. That was the only time I met him, and yet to this day I feel inclined to think of what he did as being expressive of a helpful character trait, even though I am well aware of all the other possible explanations of his action. And, as with bad-naming, my giving Byron a good name involves my assuming, without evidence, that his trait of helpfulness is robust – stable and consistent. Car broken down? Expect Byron to help (stability). Slipped over on a banana skin and sprained your ankle? Byron will be sure to come to your aid (consistency). In need of some ready cash to tide you over the weekend? Ring Byron (more consistency). And so on, across a wide range of situations where helping behaviour is appropriate.

ALL OF US ARE ROUND; NONE OF US IS FLAT

Let's return to something that we first met in Chapter 1: E. M. Forster's distinction between flat and round characters in the novel. This is what Forster says about flat characters:

> Flat characters were called 'humours' in the seventeenth century, and are sometimes called types, and sometimes caricatures. In their purest form, they are constructed round a single idea or quality; when there is more than one factor in them, we get the beginning of the curve towards the round.[5]

As Forster says, it's because flat characters have this 'single idea or quality' that they never surprise us; everything they do is determined by whatever quality or characteristic they are deemed to have, and they never act contrary to, or against, their personality. The advantage of flat characters in novels,

TV soaps and so on is that they are easily recognised by the reader or the viewer, and they are easily remembered afterwards.

We real-life human beings, in contrast, are round characters – all of us. And yet what we tend to do in our thinking is to flatten each other out – sometimes ourselves as well as others, as we will see.[6] This, as my brief review of our bad practices shows, tends to happen with others (not with ourselves) where people are fairly remote from us psychologically. Looking at people from this psychological distance, one might think of them as flat characters, but they are not; they only appear to be that way, because they are viewed from a distance so that their more subtle motivations (those of a round character) are hidden from us, or just because we simply can't be bothered to find out about them, as we couldn't be bothered to find out why our fellow guest was gloomy and morose that evening.

Forster reports the complaint of a contemporary writer, Norman Douglas, against D. H. Lawrence's flattening out of a mutual friend in a biography of him; although Douglas' remarks are aimed at flattening out in biography, they very well sum up what is wrong with our bad practices that I have been reviewing:

> It consists, I should say, in a failure to realize the profundities and complexities of the ordinary human mind; it selects for literary purposes two or three facets of a man or a woman, generally the most spectacular and therefore 'useful' ingredients of their character, and disregards all the others. Whatever fails to fit in with these specially chosen traits is eliminated; must be eliminated, for otherwise the description would not hold water. Such and such are the data; everything incompatible with those data has to go by the board.[7]

As a complaint against the novelist or the writer of a screen-play or other fictional work, I doubt that it can be made out; flattening out is often a necessary artifice, given the author's other intentions: The Magnificent Seven, Twelve Angry Men, Ten Little Indians — if all seven, twelve or ten were round, we'd just become confused as to who was who. As a complaint against biographers, I think that it often hits home. And, understood as a complaint against our ordinary everyday bad practices concerning real people, I am sure that it hits home.

Nietzsche, like Norman Douglas, thought the complaint reaches wider, and he certainly thought it hits home against our everyday bad practices with real people:

> *Created people.* When we say the dramatist (and the artist in general) actually *creates* characters, this is a nice piece of deception and exaggeration in the existence and dissemination of which art celebrates one of its unintentional and as it were superfluous triumphs. In reality we understand very little of an actual living person and generalize very superficially when we attribute to him this or that character: well, the poet adopts the same *very imperfect* posture towards man as we do, in that his sketches of men are just as *superficial* as is our knowledge of men. There is much illusion involved in these created characters of the artists; they are in no way living products of nature, but, like painted people, a little too thin, they cannot endure inspection from close to. . . And if one should even venture to say that the character of the ordinary living man is often self-contradictory and that created by the dramatist the ideal that hovered dimly before the eye of nature, this would be quite wrong.[8]

One reason, then, for flattening out real-life characters (in addition to prejudice, fear of the unknown stranger from 'abroad', and sheer laziness about the appropriate use of evidence) is the illusory desire for complete understanding of people. With this is supposed to come the elimination of the possibility of being surprised. As Jean-Paul Sartre put it, 'Who cannot see how offensive to the Other and how reassuring for me is a statement such as, "He's just a —", which removes a disturbing freedom from a trait and which aims at henceforth constituting all the acts of the Other as consequences following strictly from his essence.'[9] And finally, flattening ourselves out can often be a form of bad faith – a denial of responsibility: 'I can't help it, I'm just a —.' But, as Forster said, 'In daily life we never understand each other, neither complete clairvoyance nor complete confessional exists.'[10]

Apart from our bad practices, there are, I think, two other kinds of reason – good ones – why we ascribe robust traits to people. The first is in order to *explain and predict their thoughts, feelings and actions*. The second reason concerns our *idealism about character*; we ascribe robust character traits to others – and to ourselves – because that is how we think we *ought* to be. In order to get to grips with these reasons for our use of trait terms, and to tease apart the good practices from the bad ones, we need to turn to social psychology and to what social psychologists call *dispositionism*.

SOCIAL PSYCHOLOGY AND DISPOSITIONISM

This is what Lee Ross and Richard Nisbett, two well-known social psychologists, say about dispositionism:

> The answer we get both from research evidence and from everyday experience is that people are inveterate dispositionists. They account for past actions and outcomes, and make predictions about future actions and outcomes, in

terms of the person – or more specifically, in terms of
presumed personality traits or other distinctive and enduring
personal dispositions. The evidence . . . suggests that people
automatically – and unconsciously – provide a dispositional
interpretation to behavioural information. And it further
suggests that the dispositions they favour are suspiciously
similar to the trait constructs fabled in song, story and
personology texts . . . it suggests that people will make
confident trait-based predictions on a small evidence base
and will be unmotivated to increase their evidence base
before making predictions.[11]

The research evidence that Ross and Nisbett refer to here
shows not only that we really are inclined towards dispositional thinking (towards ascribing robust traits to others and
to ourselves), but also that dispositionism is false – there are
no such traits. There are many experiments in this field, and I
will just choose two, both of which are concerned with helping behaviour. They are, I think, independently enjoyable.[12]

Mary drops some important papers in the crowded shopping mall. Someone is making a call in a nearby phone booth
and sees what happened. Will he or she be the one who goes
to help Mary pick up her papers? According to dispositionism, it depends on whether or not he or she is a helpful
person. How people act in a given situation is determined by
their traits, so, more or less, a helpful person will help, and
someone who isn't won't; and minutiae of the situation
shouldn't affect this prediction. Let's see what happens.

This first experiment was set up so that, as the papers are
dropped in the mall (by the 'Mary' character), some of the
callers find a dime in the coin-returned slot of his or her
pay-phone and some don't. (Like most experiments in social

psychology, the whole thing was a set-up.) Result? Of those who found the dime, 14 out of 16 helped. Of those who weren't so lucky, only 1 out of 24 helped. It seems that the details of the situation are highly relevant in determining behaviour. And, given that there were no *systematic* differences in personality between the dime-finders and those who didn't find a dime, one begins to wonder whether the helping behaviour of any given individual (you, me) would similarly depend on this apparently trivial fact, and not on one's personality.

Next experiment: someone comes across an apparently injured person whom he passes by on the street. Will he or she stop to help? (Think Byron here.) Again, the disposition-ist answer is that it depends: it depends on whether or not he or she is the helping *type* – whether or not he or she has a robust helpful trait; other factors may be relevant but this is the crucial one. Let's see what happens.

The unwitting subjects of this experiment were Princeton seminarians, some of whom were asked to prepare a talk on the parable of the Good Samaritan, and some of whom were asked to prepare a talk on job prospects for seminarians. Some from each group were told that they had plenty of time to get to the other end of the campus where the talk had to be delivered, some were told they had just about enough time to get there, and some were told that they must rush in order not to be late. On the way to giving the talk, by prearrangement (another set-up), each one had to pass by on the road an apparently distressed colleague.

It turns out that the crucial factor in determining whether the seminarians stopped to help was whether or not they were in a hurry, and not what their personality traits were. Of those with plenty of time 63 per cent helped, of those with enough time 45 per cent helped, and of those in a hurry only 10 per cent helped. Whether or not the seminarian was about to give a talk on the parable of the Good Samaritan was not a significant variable. Nor was it significant whether or not (according to responses to a prior questionnaire) their interest in religion was to do primarily with helping others or with their own salvation.

Separate studies, related to this second experiment, have shown that these results are not what we ordinary folk predict, for we tend to be dispositionists. In one such study, people were asked to predict what subjects would do in a situation similar to the one just described. The prediction was that there would be a 20 percentage point gap between those whose religion was concerned with helping others and those whose religion was concerned primarily with their own salvation, and that whether or not the seminarian was in a hurry would be irrelevant in determining behaviour. Wrong on both counts. Moreover, we fail to adjust our beliefs as we should when we are wised up to the right answers: even then we still seem to continue to over-emphasise the importance of differences in traits in determining action, and underemphasise the importance of the details of the situation.[13]

So these experiments (and many, many others) seem to show both that we are prone to dispositionism, and that dispositionism is false. To be clear, this isn't to say that there is no such thing as personality or character *period*, or that people don't differ in their personality and character, although some social psychologists and some philosophers sometimes give the impression that this is what they think. But behind the headlines ('The Nonexistence of Character Traits') and the rhetoric lies a somewhat more considered view: the denial that there are *robust* traits, that is, traits that are both stable and consistent across a broad and diverse range of situations.[14]

Nevertheless, we still mustn't lose sight of just how dramatic these findings are. The practice of ascribing, to others and to ourselves, robust traits – honesty, kindness, helpfulness, friendliness and so on – is a deeply embedded part of our ordinary everyday psychological practice and moral thinking. Here, for example, is what Rosalind Hursthouse, a well-known contemporary philosopher writing on the virtues, says we can expect from an honest person:

> we expect a reliability in their actions; they do not lie or cheat or plagiarize or casually pocket other people's possessions. You can rely on them to tell you the truth, to give sincere references, to own up to their mistakes, not to pretend to be more knowledgeable than they are; you can buy a used car from them or ask for their opinion with confidence . . . we expect them in conversation to praise or defend people, real and fictitious, for their honesty, to avoid consorting with the dishonest, to choose, where possible, to work with honest people and have honest friends, to be bringing up their children to be honest . . . we expect them to uphold the ideals of truth and honesty in their jobs.[15]

EXPLAINING AND PREDICTING

Where do we go from here? What I think we need to do is to separate out different things that are at work in our dispositionism – in our propensity to ascribe robust traits to people, like the honesty that Hursthouse has just been discussing. On the one hand are our bad practices. These practices are indeed bad, and we'd be better off without them: we should avoid doing what the vulgar do. On the other hand, there are good reasons why our dispositionism (shorn, hopefully, of the bad practices) is an essential part of our everyday thinking about ourselves and others. One set of reasons concerns explanation and prediction of what people do, and another set concerns our moral thinking. They are related, but I'll begin by looking at explanation and prediction of what people do.

Actions, as we saw in Chapter 1, can be explained by reference to the motive or the reasons that the person had for doing the action, where those reasons are occurrent thoughts and feelings, which make sense of the action, or make the action intelligible, understandable or rational. (I will, controversially, take these four terms to be equivalent in meaning. In fact, I think they aren't equivalent, but the oversimplification will do no great harm here.)

We find someone's action intelligible or understandable by finding something about the action that he or she values or cares for. If Geoff goes bungee-jumping, then perhaps he likes danger – that would make it intelligible; or perhaps the girl he loves goes bungee-jumping every weekend, and it's the only way he can keep in contact with her. If Consie gives all her money to the cats' home, this would make sense if she cares greatly for cats. If Sultan Mehmet has all nineteen of his half-brothers killed the day he assumes his position as supreme ruler, then this would be the rational thing to do if he values being undisputed ruler above family relations.[16] We find these actions and activities intelligible or rational in Geoff, Consie and the Sultan because we find it intelligible that someone could have these values that explain their choices and actions, even if we don't ourselves share their values, and even if we ourselves consider them to be immoral or imprudent.

What I've done with Geoff, Consie and the Sultan is to refer to the longer-term dispositional structure of their motivations and preferences – their personality traits – to make sense of their actions and their choices. Making sense of an action or finding it intelligible, where there are several other actions that could be done (as there usually are), crucially depends on appeal to personality traits like these.[17]

Personality traits like these are reason-responsive. Liking danger, being a cat-lover and being a ruthless power-seeker are reason-responsive dispositions: danger-loving Geoff thinks that the fact that bungee-jumping will be dangerous is a reason to choose to go bungee-jumping this weekend; Consie thinks that the fact that many cats' lives will go better if she gives money to the home for cats is a reason to choose to give money to it; the Sultan thinks that the fact that his half-brothers might constitute a threat to his rule is a good reason to have them killed.

Not all personality traits are reason-responsive, but those that aren't can also be appealed to as explanations, but of behaviour, as contrasted, roughly, with action. Giggliness, for example, isn't a reason-responsive trait, but we can explain why yesterday a twelve-year old giggled by appealing to the fact that she is disposed to giggle when in company – she's a giggly person – and the fact that she was then in company. The fact that she was in company wasn't a reason for her giggling in the psychological sense of the word 'reason'; 'reason' here is more like the 'reason' why the sugar cube dissolved in hot water or the 'reason' why the vase shattered when dropped.

The crucial role of personality traits emerges even more clearly when we turn away from making sense of an action after it is done, and towards predicting what someone will do – again, where there is more than one intelligible thing that he or she could do. What will Geoff say and do if he is asked if he wants to go bungee-jumping next weekend? If you are Consie's niece, will your opening up a home for stray cats make it any more likely that Consie will leave you some money in her will? If you are one of Sultan Mehmet's half-brothers, should you worry about what he might do as soon as he attains power? In a shared world, where we are trying to predict people's actions, often out of an extraordinarily wide range of possible things that it would be intelligible or rational for them to do, we need to know about their personality traits to narrow down the options. This is not to say that we will be able to predict *precisely* what people will do. The idea of personality just enables us to narrow down the *range* of possible choices and actions – for example, Consie might choose to leave all her money to her cat rather than to the local cats' home; either choice would have been expressive of her enduring love of cats.

So we *need* to appeal to personality traits if we are to explain and predict others' actions. But doesn't this bring us straight back to the dispositionism that seemed so problematic in the light of the experiments in social psychology? It does not. For we can at the same time resolve to put to one side our bad practices, and to think with the man of sense and not with the vulgar. Our attributions of traits to others – initially perhaps robust – ought permanently to stand open to correction and refinement as our psychological distance from the other person narrows. Initially, we explain Geoff's choice of bungee-jumping for the weekend by reference to a general love of danger. Later, we find out that this love of danger doesn't extend to choosing to go bull-running in Pamplona (he's been averse to bulls ever since that nasty experience when he was twelve), nor does he choose to pursue his dangerous activities when there's a game of golf in the offing as an alternative (he prefers golf to dangerous activities). We adjust and refine our trait ascription accordingly.

This adjustment and refinement is especially obvious – and effective – when applied to those we know intimately and over a long period. There's a TV series called 'Five Things I Hate about You', in which a couple say to the camera what their partner's traits are, and we see the other partner unknowingly acting out their trait in front of the camera in the way that was predicted. This to my mind is perfect refutation for anyone who took the extreme view that there is no such thing as personality or character. In a recent programme in the series, Rob told us that his wife Jane was a show-off, was loud, can't dance, won't leave a party and loves tack; Jane told us that Rob was a harsh critic of others' work, tells the same joke every Thursday morning and has a bad memory. Jane even correctly predicted to us that, of the four items that she had asked Rob to buy in the supermarket, it would be the toothpaste that he would forget.

Traits like these are surely very stable. But they're not so obviously robust – that is both stable and consistent across a broad and diverse range of situations. We don't expect this consistency of personality traits. We wouldn't be surprised, disappointed or disapproving to find out that Geoff's danger-loving didn't extend to bull-running, or if he turned down bungee-jumping in favour of a game of golf; nor would we be if it emerged that Rob had a very good memory for football scores.

In contrast, consider kindness, which is a character trait, a virtue. Wouldn't we think less of a kind person if she were kind to most people, but not to Arabs or to old people? Wouldn't we think less of her if she turned down the opportunity to be kind to the injured stranger on her way home, because if she did stop she'd miss the beginning of *Neighbours*? The idea, then, is this. Our thinking about character traits, in contrast to our thinking about the more superficial personality traits, is *idealistic*: we think that if someone is kind, then she ought *robustly* to be kind, not failing to be kind just because the needy person is an Arab or is old, or for some trivial reason such as not missing *Neighbours*. It is to this notion – idealism – that I now turn.

IDENTIFICATION AND IDEALISM

In Chapter 1, I introduced the idea that there is something important about us humans that marks us off from other sentient creatures. We are self-conscious creatures. We also have a language. We are capable of being conscious of our own occurrent thoughts and feelings, and of our dispositional psychological traits, and of those of other people, and we can ascribe them, to ourselves and to others ('I'm feeling angry'; 'Susan is a kind person'). Other sentient creatures are possessors of occurrent thoughts and feelings, and of dispositional psychological traits; humans (adult humans) are both possessors and ascribers.

This makes our trait psychology much more complex than that of other sentient creatures. In particular, it enables us to *identify* with our own motives and traits. Your identification with a trait of yours involves your considering that trait to be, in some sense, part of who you are – part of your identity. In the sense in which I will be using the term, identification also involves considering that trait to be a good one, one that you approve of or prize, a virtue. These two elements can (and often do) come apart. For example, poor Sugar Kane (née Kowalczyk), the ukulele player in *Some Like It Hot* played by Marilyn Monroe, said of herself that she always got the fuzzy end of the lollipop: always falling for the mean, selfish tenor sax player, always the one to get caught drinking, and so on. Sugar considered herself to be a loser, thinking that being like this was part of who she was, part of her identity. But this is not identification in my sense, because she didn't prize being a loser. (She might have been fatalist about it, but that's another matter.)

If Susan identifies with her character trait of kindness, considering it a virtue, she will be *idealistic* about it: she will consider that she ought to be robustly – stably and consistently – kind, even if she isn't fully virtuous and is occasionally tempted to act selfishly, and not to do what a kind person ought to do. She is, in precisely this sense, a dispositionist about her own kindness, just as Rosalind Hursthouse suggested in her remarks about what we expect in an honest person. Susan is not a dispositionist because she is at a psychological distance from herself. And she's not a dispositionist as part of a bad practice, or out of Sartrean bad faith. No, her dispositionism about herself is a form of idealism – being robustly kind is what she thinks she *ought* to be, where this 'ought' is idealistic and moral as well as predictive.

Now I want to put flesh on these bones, by considering a deceptively simple everyday example.

THE THIRD GLASS OF CHAMPAGNE

Temperance was on Aristotle's list of virtues. And it is a virtue. It has got something of a bad name these days – temperance societies and so on – partly because the idea of temperance now suggests abstinence. But temperance really is the disposition to partake of pleasures of drink, food and sex *appropriately*, or as one ought: as Aristotle puts it, in the now familiar phrase, in the right amount, at the right time, in the right way, with the right feelings, with the right people, and so on. So, in this sense of temperance (the correct one), the appropriate amount of alcohol to consume could be a lot; if you were on your best friend's stag weekend in Amsterdam, it would not be temperate in this sense (the correct one) to have a small glass of champagne before dinner and then stick to water.

Now to the example. You're at a cocktail party. In these circumstances, let's say that the appropriate amount to drink is two glasses of champagne. This is the temperate thing to do; more than two would be intemperate. You have two glasses. Then your host comes round and offers you a refill. What will you do? Will you take the offer of the refill or will you decline?

The lesson of the last few pages is, I hope, that the answer to this question will depend on your character – on what sort of person you are. Let's assume that you're temperate and that you identify with your temperance, prizing it and considering it to be part of who you are. So, when you're offered the refill, you see that this is an offer that you *ought* to refuse. But you're tempted: you want a third glass of that delicious champagne (it looks even more delicious after the second glass), and that's *why* you're tempted. But you know that you ought to refuse, and that is what you've resolved to do.

We've all been there. You need strength of will to do what you know you ought to do when you are tempted to do otherwise. This is why we only need strength of will if we are less than fully virtuous, for strength of will is needed only when we are tempted, and the fully virtuous person is never tempted. Strength of will is for this reason sometimes called an 'executive virtue': it isn't really a full virtue because the fully virtuous person doesn't need it. It involves a whole collection or parcel of techniques and skills that help the less than fully virtuous person, on the road to virtue, to do (to 'execute') what he knows he ought to do.[18]

The fully temperate person is at the end of the road to virtue. She is the *ideal*, which none of us (apart from the very odd exception) ever attains. Such a person fully identifies with temperance, and has the ideally robust disposition, to have the right thoughts and feelings, and to act as she should. Being fully virtuous, she has the *appropriate* desires for pleasure (in this case wanting two glasses of champagne *and no more*), so she is never tempted to stray from virtue.

In the imagined situation, you also identify with temperance, but, being less than fully virtuous, you feel the pull of desires that are out of line with what you know that temperance requires: in this case you feel the pull of a desire for a third glass of champagne. Nevertheless, let's say you're strong-willed, so – at least on this occasion – you actually do what you know you ought to do. You might think to yourself something like 'It's very tempting, but I really ought to refuse.' The next time you're in a similarly tempting situation, we can be pretty certain that you will again decide to refuse, and you will again be tempted. But what will you *do* next time? Will your strength of will get you through again? We can't be sure, and nor can you.

Then there is the weak-willed person (you next time?). Like you, he identifies with temperance, and, like you, he is tempted. But – at least on this occasion – he lacks the strength of will to do what he knows he ought. So he gives way to temptation and takes the third glass. He too might think to himself, 'It's very tempting, but I really ought to refuse', but he fails to act on what he resolves to do. Aristotle very nicely says, of the weak-willed drinker, that he recites the verses of Empedocles as he has one more drink than he should have, the point of the remark being that the verses of Empedocles were about the benefits of temperance.[19] Such a person, Aristotle says, in another helpful remark, is 'like a city that votes for all the right decrees and has good laws, but does not apply them'.[20] He will regret his failure to be temperate on this occasion. But, being idealist – and thus dispositionist – about his temperance, he doesn't qualify his ascription.

Next in the imagined situation is the intemperate person. She is not conflicted. She desires as many glasses of champagne as she can manage to drink in one evening; physical capacity is her only restraint. Having a third glass is what she decides to do, and this is what she does. And she has no regrets afterwards. Aristotle, comparing the weak-willed and the intemperate, said, in effect, that at least the weak-willed person makes the right choice, even if he doesn't act on it.[21]

That just about completes the list, apart from what Aristotle calls the 'bestial' person, bestiality being 'less grave than vice but more frightening'. (Aristotle also says that it's 'most often found in foreigners'.[22]) So, gladly leaving the bestial person to one side, we can summarise the motivational structures and actions of these four people on being offered the refill – the third glass of champagne (see table below).

With this example before us, even though it's extremely simple, we can already see what a mistake it is to 'operationalise' action, into, in this example, a simple either/or of accepting/refusing the refill. Thus operationalised, we only have two kinds of 'action'. But the motivational structures of all four types are very different. Moreover, once you look at the detail of what they do, their actions, viewed from close up, will typically reveal whether or not they are tempted. The two who are tempted both seem hesitant; their eyes dwell longingly on the champagne that is being offered to them; they

Personality type	What does he or she choose to do?	Is he or she tempted to do other than what is chosen?	What does he or she in fact do?
Fully temperate	To refuse the refill	No	Refuse the refill
Temperate but not fully, and strong-willed	To refuse the refill	Yes	Refuse the refill
Temperate but not fully, and weak-willed	To refuse the refill	Yes	Accept the refill
Intemperate	To accept the refill	No	Accept the refill

might say yes, and then no, and then yes. You can *see* them being tempted. The other two look more certain and sure of what they're doing, not being tempted to do other than what they have decided to do.

This is not to say that another person's motives are utterly transparent from their actions, closely observed in all their details (as Forster said, 'complete clairvoyance' doesn't exist). And your own motives can often be opaque to you, however much you search your own soul ('complete confessional' doesn't exist either). As you accept the offer of the third glass, you might ask yourself whether you are being weak-willed or intemperate; perhaps on occasions like this one, you *used* to be weak-willed, but now you are becoming intemperate, even though you still say the sorts of things that the weak-willed person says ('I really shouldn't you know, but it's been a long hard day'). You are deceiving yourself: you are on the road to vice, not on the road to virtue. This *opacity* of our own motivational structures will lead me in Chapter 4 to put forward another executive virtue, in addition to strength of will: *circumspection*.

THE ROAD TO VIRTUE AND THE FRAGILITY OF CHARACTER

For most of us the road to virtue is not a road that will end in our actually being fully virtuous. Kant reflected with great sensitivity on this, and on the struggle that we humans, less than fully virtuous, have to face. For him, as we saw in Chapter 2, the struggle is between duty and inclination. On my story, following Aristotle in this respect, the struggle is between the demands of the virtue that we identify with, and the pull of our other desires which run contrary to virtue: in the case of temperance these desires are for pleasure (for that extra glass of champagne); with courage, they will be for self-preservation; with benevolence and honesty, they will be self-regarding desires (or perhaps just indifference and sloth). Life is, Kant says, an 'everlasting struggle'. Whilst 'the true strength of virtue is a tranquil mind with a considered and firm resolution to put the law of virtue into practice', in us human beings 'virtue is always in progress'. 'Complete conformity of the will with the moral law is . . . a perfection of which no rational being of the sensible world [in other words no human being] is capable at any moment of his existence'; all we humans can hope for is 'endless progress'.[23]

And yet we are idealistic about character – part of our more general idealism about morality. Where we identify with our own kindness, our helpfulness, our temperance, our courageousness, we take them to be robust traits. When the moment arises for action, we resolve or set ourselves to act as we know we ought to. But, as we all know from our own experience, the test of the firmness of a resolution is in the actual ability to put it into practice. And here so often we fail, being less than perfectly virtuous, and lacking the requisite strength of will. And we then blame ourselves for our failures, perhaps completely withdrawing the ascription of the virtue to ourselves, or even ascribing the contrary vice, rather than qualifying or refining the virtue ascription.

We are similarly idealistic about other people's virtues. We attribute virtues to other people such as kindness, generosity, courage and so on, and then expect them to *be* kind, generous, brave, and to be able to withstand all sorts of everyday pressures and temptations that the contingent circumstances of life throw their way. Then, armed with this idealism, we take a failure to act as virtue requires to imply a lack of the virtue, or even the presence of the contrary vice (give a dog a bad name). Idealism about the powers of human beings in general (doubted, as we saw, by Kant) thus leads to disappointment about the motivations of a particular human being, and to blame. This idealism – a kind of optimism really – comes over very clearly to me in people's predictions about what the seminarians would do. People predicted that being in a hurry wouldn't affect whether or not the seminarian would help the distressed person; and they predicted this because that is how they think the seminarians *ought* to act. The moral 'ought' and the predictive 'ought' thus coincide in our idealism about character.

WHERE WE'VE GOT TO AND WHERE WE'RE GOING

We have tendencies – bad practices I've called them – to flatten each other out. Moreover, we tend to treat others as if their motivations find their source in robust character traits – dispositionism. Experiments in social psychology, such as the two that I have considered here, have shown both that we are prone to dispositionism, and that dispositionism is not an accurate picture of our *actual* psychology. In spite of these conclusions, I've tried to show that trait thought and talk play a central role in our making sense of and predicting others' actions, as well as in our moral thinking, where it represents a kind of idealism about people's motivations and abilities to do what they know they ought to do, according to the character traits with which they identify. Morally, we expect more of people – including ourselves – than is realistic. So whilst dispositionism isn't an accurate picture of our actual psychology, its role in our moral thinking remains as an ideal by which we guide our own actions, and by which we judge the actions of others.

Failure to live up to our ideals leads to moral criticism. This is what happened to Jim in Joseph Conrad's *Lord Jim*. At a crucial moment in his life, Jim failed to do the courageous thing that he knew he ought to do. And for the rest of his life he blamed himself for it. I will begin the next chapter with Jim's story, using it as a pointer to some of the lessons that we can learn about the fragility of character. This will then take us to the question of responsibility for our character.

Four

RESPONSIBILITY AND FRAGILITY

In Chapter 2, I discussed the importance of motive and character in our moral evaluation of action. Byron, you will recall, rescued me when I was stranded, and our evaluation of what he did depended in part on his reasons for doing what he did, and on the sort of person he was. The importance of motive and character came out again in Chapter 3, in my champagne example of how two people can do the same thing, but for very different kinds of motive and out of very different kinds of character trait.

I want to explore two things in this chapter. The first is moral responsibility for motive and character. If someone is ruthlessly cruel, we hold him morally responsible for being that way – for having that trait; we don't just hold him morally responsible for the ruthlessly cruel things that he does. This is a fact about what we do. But is it *right* for us to do this? How can we properly hold someone morally responsible for something that isn't in his direct control – that might be a trait that he inherited from his parents (who, in Philip Larkin's words, 'fill you with the faults they had, And add some extra just for you')?

The second thing I want to explore is the lessons that we can learn from our consideration of the fragility of character. The central lesson will be that circumspection about our own motives and character is, like strength of will, an executive virtue. We'll hear what some great psychologists said about these things, before social psychology was a science: Nietzsche, Musil, St Augustine, Homer, and Joseph Conrad's narrator and student of human nature, Marlow.

JIM AND THE CAPTAIN

To put flesh on the bones, I'll take two characters from Conrad's Lord Jim: Jim, and Jim's Captain on his fateful voyage.[1] This book is all about character. Jim, the son of a country parson, went to sea at a young age, full of thoughts of how courageous he would be. 'He saw himself saving people from sinking ships, cutting away masts in a hurricane, swimming through a surf with a line . . . always an example of devotion to duty, and as unflinching as a hero in a book' (p. 5). He takes a berth as chief mate of a seedy, old, rusty, run-down steamer, the Patna, of dubious ownership, and captained by 'a sort of renegade New South Wales German', who 'brutalized all those he was not afraid of, and wore a "blood-and-iron" air, combined with a purple nose and a red moustache' (p. 10). Before setting off on the fateful voyage, they take on board 800 Muslims on pilgrimage to Mecca. 'Look at dese cattle', the Captain says.

One calm night, the Patna steams over a submerged wreck, and comes to a halt, with the rusty old iron bulkhead massively damaged under water, and looking as if it's going to split at any moment. The pilgrims don't know what has happened and remain quiet, but the white crew – four of them, including Jim and the Captain – see the danger. There are hardly any lifeboats, and if there were a general rush to escape, all would probably perish. The rest of the crew begin to get one of the boats off the chocks. 'Aren't you going to do something?' Jim asks, and the Captain replies with a snarl 'Yes. Clear out.' After a fierce struggle, they get the lifeboat into the water. Jim hesitates, then jumps, or almost passively falls into the boat; 'I knew nothing about it till I looked up', said Jim later, to Conrad's narrator, Marlow.

The Patna doesn't sink, and all the pilgrims are saved, no thanks to the four escapees, who are picked up and taken to Bombay for a naval hearing. The Captain flees brazen-facedly, but Jim stays to face the music, and loses his licence. He is disgraced. And for the rest of the novel Jim moves from eastern seaport to eastern seaport, trying to keep one step ahead of his reputation.

Now, Jim and the Captain did the same thing. Each deserted a ship that he thought was about to sink, leaving on board 800 pilgrims to what he thought was a certain death. There is no doubt that this was a terrible thing to have done. But my interest here is not directly in what they did, but rather in the motivations and states of character and will which lie behind and serve to explain their actions. The Captain, as we will see, acted out of a bad character, and the question of moral responsibility will revolve around whether the Captain (and others like him with bad character traits) is responsible for being the way he is. Then I will turn to Jim, who, in contrast, acted not out of a bad character but out of a weak-willed failure to act as he knew he ought – in accordance with his own ideals of duty and courage. The lessons we can draw from Jim's experiences will lead us to a discussion of the idea of being circumspect about our own motives and character.

DODGING DIRECT RESPONSIBILITY FOR A BAD CHARACTER

As a matter of fact, we do hold people directly responsible morally for their character traits. We hold the Captain directly responsible morally for being a cowardly bully: we reproach or condemn him for being the way he is. The question is whether or not we are right to do so. And there is a beguilingly simple argument that is supposed to show that we are not – that we cannot justifiably hold people directly responsible for having a bad character trait.

The argument goes like this:

1. We're only properly held directly responsible morally for what is in our direct voluntary control, for what we can bring about by directly trying. We can thus be held directly responsible for our actions and omissions because they are in our direct control. Try, right now, to move your arm! There, you did it – your arm moved. And you did this action *just like that*, just by directly trying.

2. Having a particular character trait is not within our direct voluntary control in this sense; we can't change our character traits *just like that*, by directly trying. Try, right now, to be a kinder person! Have you done it yet – are you kinder already? Surely not yet. When Twiggy said that her motto is 'be kind, loyal and true', she didn't mean that all you need to do is try and it'll happen, just like that, straight away.[2]

3. Therefore we cannot be properly held directly responsible for our character traits.

This argument is certainly valid – the conclusion follows from the two premises. So, if one wants to resist the conclusion, as I do, one must consider whether or not the premises are true.

What about the second premise? Can we deny this, and say that we can change our character traits just like that? To say this would be to fly in the face of our ordinary way of thinking about character traits. Moreover, it would be to fly in the face of what I have been saying character is. Character traits are relatively enduring, and, as we saw in Chapter 2, it takes time and practice – habituation – for them to become embedded in our psychology; so they can't be adopted, or got rid of, just like that, just by trying. So, although I will have quite a lot more to say later – especially in Chapter 5 – about how we can change our character traits over time, partly through directly trying to do other things, the second premise does seem right: character traits aren't within our direct voluntary control in the way that actions are, such as your action of moving your arm.

So let's look at the first premise. If we accept this premise, and the rest of the argument, we should realise that there will be other kinds of states of mind that fall outside the scope of direct moral responsibility: not just character traits, but beliefs, emotions, and long-term attachments to things and to people, for all of these seem not to be in our direct voluntary control either. And yet we do hold people directly responsible morally for their racist beliefs, for feeling envious of their colleagues' successes, for loving their cats more than they love their children. So, even though the argument is beguiling, we should appreciate that it would have wide ramifications if we were to accept it.

What the proponent of the argument does at this stage, to block these counter-intuitive ramifications, is to say that what we really do in such cases is hold people *indirectly* responsible. According to their argument, we can't be held *directly* responsible for having a morally bad character trait. But still, they add, we can be held *indirectly* responsible for our character, to the extent that we're responsible for its causes. So, according to this view, the Captain of the *Patna*, a cruel and cowardly person, isn't directly responsible for being a cruel and cowardly person now. But he is directly responsible for his past actions or omissions, for having done, and failed to do, things that have caused him now to be cruel and cowardly. And thus responsibility for character is only indirect – going via his past actions and omissions. And the same goes for beliefs, emotions and long-term attachments.

This indirect way of making people morally responsible for their character is, I think, to be resisted. There is a view at work here which we need to get to the bottom of: the view that moral responsibility for all kinds of psychological states (beliefs, emotions, attachments, character traits) should be reduced to, or turned into, moral responsibility for actions and omissions.[3]

So I think it's the first premise we should doubt. And thinking more about the indirect route to moral responsibility for character should reinforce this doubt. Consider a woman who is a profoundly envious person, especially of others' material possessions and successes. She is even envious of the successes of her friends. But she doesn't know that she is. Should she, in the past, have done things to make herself a less envious person? But how could she have done, given her ignorance of her envy? So perhaps she should have known that she was envious, and she should have done things to find out about her ignorance? But perhaps we can trace this ignorance back to some other trait that is not within her direct voluntary control, and that she is not aware of; perhaps she is greedy for money, and doesn't know it. So it looks as if the person who wants to make us only indirectly responsible for our character traits will find that, in some cases, it won't be possible to pin the responsibility on any particular past voluntary action or omission. And when one thinks about our bad character traits, many of them are like this woman's envy. We don't realise we are self-righteous, inconsiderate, thoughtless, ungenerous and so on. But why should our ignorance get us off the hook?

One of the important consequences of the position that I'm advocating, of our being *directly* responsible for our bad character traits (and for our lacking certain good traits), is the way it affects our attitudes towards our own character. If I am envious, or inconsiderate, or ungenerous, I should accept responsibility for it, and reproach myself for being the way I am. And accepting responsibility like this is often the first step towards doing the things that might put me right. But my responsibility isn't *just* to do these things. My responsibility – my direct responsibility – is for being the way I am – for being this kind of person.

THE SCORPION AND THE FROG

But now the following worry arises, which I think is often behind the rejection of my position. Surely we are often not to blame for our character traits because they are the result of a bad upbringing, or of some other factor in our past lives, inheritance perhaps, that was not our 'fault' (the Larkin point). That woman's envy of her friends' material successes might have come about because she was the child of grasping, materially minded parents. So it's not her fault. The nature–nurture debate – how much of her envy is due to genetic inheritance and how much to upbringing and environment – is irrelevant; either way, it's not her fault. (In fact, there are very persuasive arguments that it is *senseless* to ask, in respect of any individual person, how much of any given trait is due to genetic factors and how much to environment.[4])

In a version of one of Aesop's fables, a scorpion and a frog both want to cross the river. As the scorpion can't swim, it asks the frog to give it a ride on its back. 'But won't you sting me?' asks the frog. 'Of course I won't', says the scorpion, 'for if I did, I would drown as well as you.' So they set off across the stream with the scorpion on the frog's back. Half-way across, the scorpion stings the frog. Paralysed and sinking fast, the frog cries out, 'But why? Now we will both drown.' 'I'm sorry', says the scorpion, 'I couldn't help it. It's in my nature.'

It can be very relieving to think that you aren't responsible for being the way you are, and instead to blame your past, your heritage, your upbringing, your parents, your genes. This, I think, is part of the attraction of the position about moral responsibility that I reject. It gets you off the hook. My approach is that, in taking direct responsibility for being the way you are – for your character traits – and reproaching yourself for these traits if they're bad ones, you are already in a position to start to try to be better. The expression 'owning up' is a nice one here: not in the sense of confessing, but in the sense of accepting some trait *as your own* (remember, though, that this isn't the same as identifying with a trait).

In a sense, though, the scorpion is right. It's right *because it is a scorpion*, and scorpions aren't responsible for their actions or for their 'character' – their dispositions. We – we humans – are different, and this is the point of the fable. We humans can't excuse all our morally bad actions because they are expressive of traits of character that aren't our fault because they are 'in our nature'.

Let's apply this to the Captain in *Lord Jim*. According to my approach, we rightly hold him directly responsible morally for being the cruel, cowardly, heartless person that he is. But what if the Captain had been brought up by a brutalising father? Should we reproach or censure him less than if his vicious traits arose through his own voluntary actions? Perhaps. (I return to this point later.) Nevertheless, my point remains that, however our states of character have been arrived at, regardless of their causes, they are our responsibility, and we should own up to them – make them our own. It's so easy to say what the scorpion said, that it's not our fault.

THE SCOPE OF MORAL RESPONSIBILITY

Someone, like my opponent, who wants to resist the idea that we are directly responsible for our character traits, has another move to make at this point. 'Where is the limit to moral responsibility?' she rhetorically asks. 'If I am morally responsible for character traits that I didn't voluntarily bring about in myself, why aren't I also morally responsible and to be reproached for any psychological trait that is a disposition to do morally bad things? Is there no limit to moral responsibility?'

The challenge is a fair one. To respond, what I need to do is to make out a fundamental difference between talent and virtue, and between defect and vice, and to show how this difference grounds a special kind of emotional response or attitude towards character traits – towards virtues and vices.

Let's look at some emotional responses, or 'reactive attitudes' as Sir Peter Strawson calls them in his justly famous paper, 'Freedom and resentment'. The table below shows some, of the negative variety.[5]

Let's concentrate to begin with on just our negative below-the-line reactive attitudes towards others – the bottom right-hand box. We could say this: if (and only if) it's appropriate to hold X morally responsible for Y, then it's appropriate to have one of these reactive attitudes towards X in respect of Y. Then, in rising to the challenge to say what the scope or reach of

Towards oneself	Towards another
Shame	Disgust
Humility	Derision
Embarrassment	Contempt
	Scorn
	Mockery
Guilt	Reproach
Blame (of oneself)	Blame
Remorse	Resentment
Regret	Indignation
Compunction	Condemnation
	Censure

moral responsibility is, we need to say what are the X's and the Y's. Let's start with the X's.

Inanimate objects and non-human animals don't fall into this category as potential objects of moral responsibility *at all*. Although you might blame the weather for spoiling the picnic, or the dog for knocking over the vase, this is (or ought to be) just a matter of attributing *causal* responsibility. That's why the scorpion was right about itself: it's not to be blamed for anything – for being disposed to sting frogs, or for the action of stinging this particular frog. Children below a certain age are (or ought to be) also exempt from moral responsibility and thus from these reactive attitudes. So too are (or ought to be) those who are mentally ill and cannot tell the difference between right and wrong – sociopaths for example.[6] It's really only *rational persons* about whom these attitudes are in principle appropriate. So the Captain of the *Patna* is not in principle exempt from moral responsibility, for he is a rational person, and knows the difference between right and wrong.

What can the X's (rational persons we now know) be held morally responsible for? What is the scope of the Y's? Well, there are actions – rational people can be properly held morally responsible for what they do. The Captain is morally responsible for abandoning what he thought was a sinking ship. But the issue here is whether rational persons can properly be held directly responsible morally for their character traits. Can the Captain be morally responsible for being such a brutal coward, and is it appropriate to condemn him for it?

I think that the heart of the matter is this: rational people are morally responsible only for those of their traits which are reason-responsive, as are all character traits. Thus, reactive attitudes that are below the horizontal line in the table are appropriate here, but not in respect of personality traits that are not reason-responsive.[7] Let me explain.

Character traits, I said in Chapter 2, are reason-responsive: dispositions reliably to respond to certain kinds of reasons. Good character traits – virtues – are dispositions to respond to certain kinds of good reasons: generous people reliably respond to reasons to be generous, and so on. Bad character traits – vices – are (roughly) dispositions to respond to certain kinds of bad reasons: cowardly people typically run to save their own skin; intemperate people reliably choose to eat or drink more than they should, and so on. So if someone has a vice, he or she is reason-responsive in what I will call this *weak sense*, which is pretty much just being rational – being capable of doing certain kinds of things for certain kinds of reasons (whether morally good or bad). So when we blame the Captain for being such a brutal coward, we are in effect blaming him for being responsive (disposed to respond) to morally bad reasons. Just so long as someone's trait is reason-responsive in this weak sense, then we are justified in holding him or her morally responsible in respect of that trait.

Now, there's a further sense in which character traits are reason-responsive. Someone with a morally bad character trait, a vice, is capable of responding to reasons to change – to reasons to cease to have the bad trait that he or she has. We need to be careful with the 'capable' here. Of course the Captain may be terribly set in his cowardly, brutish ways, failing to see any good reason at all to change. And yet this is not to say that he is *incapable* of change, so that he comes to be disposed to respond to good reasons (having the virtue) rather than bad ones (having the vice). *Something* or *someone* might persuade him to see that the road to virtue is an inviting one, and that he really ought to change his ways.

All character traits are like this – open to reason, one might say. Some personality traits are, and some aren't – some aren't reason-responsive in the weak sense. And, if a personality trait isn't reason-responsive, such as the defect of having a bad memory, then people aren't directly responsible for it, and below-the-line attitudes aren't appropriate. I might be ashamed of my bad memory, and you might mock me for it – both above-the-line attitudes – but guilt and reproach are inappropriate here. This remains the case even if the non-reason-responsive trait is a disposition to do morally bad things. Tourette's syndrome involves a disposition to utter obscenities, kleptomania a disposition to steal. These are medical conditions, not reason-responsive dispositions. Having Tourette's syndrome and being a kleptomaniac aren't *vices*. The attachment of moral responsibility to people isn't justified in respect of such traits, so it's not appropriate to have below-the-line reactive attitudes towards them for being this way (even if the people with the traits are rational in other respects).

In Sicily, during the Second World War, General Patton was

visiting his wounded and sick troops in hospital (the incident is shown in the film, *Patton*, with Patton played by George C. Scott). Patton came to the bed of a soldier who was suffering from shell-shock. Furious, Patton slapped the soldier's face and called him a coward. We can see on my account just why Patton was wrong to react as he did. Having shell-shock, like having Tourette's syndrome, is not a reason-responsive disposition, and Patton was deeply mistaken to accuse the soldier of cowardice. Patton was rightly reprimanded by General Eisenhower and was obliged to make a public apology.

These examples show that my account isn't *conventionalist*: it doesn't accept as necessarily correct our current conventions of attributing moral responsibility, whatever they happen to be. Before shell-shock was recognised as a medical condition, I am sure soldiers were accused of cowardice, and reviled for it, when they shouldn't have been. Perhaps today, a better medical understanding of some other conditions will reveal that we are equally mistaken to hold people responsible for them. Perhaps today we are only beginning to realise just how much a childhood of abuse and neglect can affect a person, leaving them psychologically damaged to an extent that holding them morally responsible for their traits is not appropriate: their moral condition is no more open to reason or reason-responsive than is Tourette's syndrome or shell-shock.

It's the medical facts that matter. I mentioned in Chapter 3 the idea that flattening yourself out can be a form of bad faith – scorpion-like, you say, 'It's not my fault, I can't help it, I'm just a —.' An extreme version of this is to claim, insincerely, that your vice – your reason-responsive trait – is really just a medical condition, and to hide behind this as an excuse ('You must understand, my analyst tells me I am very ill'). Being disposed to 'have the vapours' was in many respects the ultimate Sartrean condition of bad faith.

BACK TO IDEALISM

Another feature to my account is that it reveals another aspect of our idealism in our thinking about character traits, and in our thinking about morality generally. We are idealistic in the sense that we want the force of morality to extend to *everyone*: not just to those who consider themselves (more or less) to be moral, but also to people like the Captain – to people who have no truck with ordinary morality.

This kind of view is in disagreement with many moral philosophers, who take a position that's considerably less idealistic than mine. For example, Gilbert Harman, whom we met in another context in Chapter 3, espouses a kind of moral relativism, where the standards and norms of morality only extend to those who, in some sense, subscribe to them. So, according to Harman, someone like the Captain, or Hitler (one of Harman's examples), is 'beyond the pale' of morality – an evocative term here, because a pale is a kind of ring fence. Thus, according to Harman, we can't say, of Hitler, that he ought not to have been the way he was, a dangerous racist.[8]

Whereas, according to my view, we *can* say of Hitler that he ought not to have been the way he was, as we can of anyone who is reason-responsive in the weak sense, and who is capable – over time, not *just like that* – of becoming better. (Of course, it's possible – although I think unlikely – that Hitler was an insane sociopath; if so, we should just think of him as someone to be 'dealt with', without condemning him for being like that, or for doing what he did.) There is, in my idealistic view of what our moral thinking is, always the possibility of using reason to *reach out* to someone, however dissolute they may be. No one is beyond the pale; or, to be precise, no rational person is beyond the pale in respect of their reason-responsive dispositions.

Isn't this morality far too demanding of others? In particular, doesn't it mean that we should go around holding people morally responsible and blaming or censuring them for their bad character traits, when they have not been brought up to know any better, or when they are ignorant of their vices? There are four points I would like to make in reply.

First, expressing your reactive attitudes towards someone, and telling him that you hold him morally responsible, is often not going to be the best approach to getting him to see reason. The idea is ridiculous that we should go around prodding people in the chest, saying, 'I reproach you for being the way you are! You ought not to be like this!', and it's no part of my view.

Secondly, it's helpful in this context, as I mentioned earlier, to remember the importance of holding *yourself* morally responsible for your character. It is often only through doing this, and through realising that you could be otherwise, that the road to becoming a better person can be set out on in the right spirit. As Robert Adams says,

> the struggle against a wrong state of mind in oneself is normally a form of *repentance*, which involves self-reproach. At the centre of such a process is one's *taking responsibility* for one's state of mind . . . whereas if one says, 'I'm not to blame for my ingratitude because I can't help it,' one takes some of the pressure off oneself by seeking refuge in an excuse.[9]

My third point is that our below-the-line reactive attitudes towards people's character traits should be a matter of degree. For example, I think that more reproach is appropriate towards a middle-class European or American man who today is disposed to have sexist and racist attitudes, than towards such a man who had the same kinds of attitudes in the 1830s. This isn't because it was less *wrong* or less *bad* to have sexist and racist attitudes in the 1830s. The point, rather, is that the reasons for not being sexist and racist are more readily available to someone today than they were then. Someone today ought to know better.[10] Someone in the 1830s ought to have known better too, of course, but the reasons for being otherwise were less available to him. Holding someone morally responsible is compatible with understanding and forgiveness.

Fourthly and finally, there needn't be any direct relation between holding someone morally responsible for something and punishing them for it. I myself think people shouldn't be punished for their morally bad character, or for their morally bad beliefs or emotions, or for anything that isn't within their direct voluntary control. Once we've put punishment entirely to one side in this area, we can see more clearly the importance and the appropriateness of holding people, including oneself, directly responsible morally for their bad character traits.[11]

UNDERSTANDING JIM: MORAL LUCK AND MISDIRECTED FEELINGS

The Captain, then, is morally responsible for being a cruel, callous person. What about Jim, who, after all, did the same thing as the Captain?

There is idealisation here too. Jim identified with his courage, with his aspirations to do the right things, idealising himself in his imagination to be 'as unflinching as a hero in a book'. And yet, at this crucial moment in his life, he was tested, and he failed. He never forgave himself for his failure. Let's try to understand Jim and what happened to him.

Jim wanted to be able to think of himself as fully virtuous, not tempted to do other than what courage requires, not tempted by such things as fear for his own life. But Jim, like most of us, was less than completely brave. He *was* tempted, and he did act to save his own life.

Not only was Jim swayed by the thought that he would surely drown if he didn't jump into the lifeboat. He was also swayed by the terrible behaviour of the other three white members of the crew. One has, as reader of the novel, a clear impression that if Jim had been mate on a ship with good men as captain and as fellow officers, he wouldn't have done what he did. He would have done what duty required. His virtue would have been what social psychologists call 'socially sustained'.[12]

What we find here is what the contemporary philosopher Thomas Nagel has called circumstantial moral luck.[13] As Marlow said, 'there are things – they look small enough sometimes too – by which some of us are totally and completely undone' (p. 32). But what an extreme test Jim had to face! Who, we might wonder, would have been strong and courageous enough to withstand it? To quote the wise Marlow again, 'Let no soul know, for the truth can be wrung out of us only by some cruel, little, awful, catastrophe' (p. 236).

No one reproached Jim more than he reproached himself. From the awful moment of his failure – what he considered to be his act of cowardice, and I consider to be his act of weakness – he thought that others saw him as he saw himself. He tortured himself, digging at his memories as one digs at an infected tooth with one's tongue, unable to imagine that others – including Marlow – cared for him, *knowing what he had done.* Even in his final hiding place from others' knowledge, deep in the Sumatran jungle, Jim's guilty secret was kept from the woman he loved, and who loved him.

Jim clearly goes too far in his obsessive remorse and self-condemnation. Moreover, his feelings are subtly *misdirected*, in remorsefully – and remorselessly – *looking backwards*, back to that one moment in his life, that one moment of failure. Without dodging responsibility, and without avoiding reproaching himself, he could have focused his thoughts not, remorsefully, on the past, and on what he did wrong at that single, fateful moment, but on the future, and on changing himself so that he wouldn't make the same mistake again. As Nietzsche so brilliantly put it: 'Never yield to remorse, but at once tell yourself: remorse would simply mean adding to the first act of stupidity a second. – If we have done harm we should give thought to how we can do good.'[14]

Jim was undone 'totally and completely', by circumstantial moral luck: his circumstances exposed the fragility of his character, and strength of will was not enough to get him through. What lessons can we learn, from Jim's experiences and from the discussion of the last two chapters, about how to live our own lives?

THE OPACITY OF INTROSPECTION: NIETZSCHE AND MUSIL

The first lesson is that the real springs of human action are a mystery, as much to ourselves as to others, and sometimes more so. Because we have names for things – 'motive', 'deciding', 'willing' and so on – we conclude that there is something very clear and precise that the names stand for. We may be able to deliberate about our motives, decide what to do, and later explain or make sense of what we have done – using names for motives, for deciding, for willing. But still, as Nietzsche says:

at the moment when we finally do act, our action is often enough determined by a different species of motives than the species here under discussion, those involved in our 'picture of the consequences'. What here comes into play is the way we habitually expend our energy; or some slight instigation from a person whom we fear or honour or love; or our indolence, which prefers to do what lies closest to hand; or an excitation of our imagination brought about at the decisive moment by some immediate, very trivial event; quite incalculable physical influences come into play; caprice and waywardness come into play; some emotion or other happens quite by chance to leap forth; in short, there come into play motives in part unknown to us, in part known very ill, which we can *never* take account of *beforehand* ... though I certainly learn what I finally *do*, I do not learn which motive has therewith actually proved victorious. *But we are accustomed to exclude* all these unconscious processes from the accounting and to reflect on the preparation for an act only to the extent that it is conscious; and we thus confuse conflict of motives with comparison of the possible consequences of different actions – a confusion itself very rich in consequences and one highly fateful for the evolution of morality![15]

One might think that Nietzsche had in mind the experiments in social psychology of Chapter 3 when he wrote that. And in fact social psychology has a term for the phenomenon that Nietzsche is pointing towards: confabulation. It is well documented.[16] In confabulation, we don't intentionally lie about our motives (although that is, of course, possible). We just get them wrong, because our real, underlying motivations are opaque to us. We aren't consciously aware of them. 'Consciousness is surface', said Nietzsche, anticipating Freud here as he so often did.[17]

In addition to the opacity of our motives, there is the mystery of the connection between motives and action: the mystery of willing. As the writer and diarist Robert Musil saw, one should even be mystified about willing to turn over in bed. He says this in his diaries:

> I have never caught myself in the act of willing. It was always the case that I saw only the thought – for example when I'm lying on one side in bed: now you ought to turn yourself over. This thought goes marching on in a state of complete equality with a whole set of other ones: for example, your foot is starting to feel stiff, the pillow is getting hot, etc. It is still a proper act of reflection; but it is still far from breaking out into a deed. On the contrary, I confirm with a certain consternation that, despite these thoughts, I still haven't turned over.
>
> As I admonish myself that I ought to do so and see that this does not happen, something akin to depression takes possession of me, albeit a depression that is at once scornful and resigned. And then, all of a sudden, and always in an unguarded moment, I turn over. As I do so, the first thing that I am conscious of is the movement as it is actually being performed, and frequently a memory that this started out from some part of the body or other, from the feet, for example, that moved a little, or were unconsciously shifted, from where they had been lying, and that they then drew all the rest after them.[18]

Many of our actions are like this: you are willing and willing to do something, and then suddenly there you are – doing it: kissing her for the first time, refusing the third glass of champagne, saying what you really think to your boss. Jim said, after his fateful leap, that he knew nothing about his jumping until he 'found himself' in the lifeboat; as Marlow put it, it had happened somehow (p. 81), it was more like being pushed than it was like jumping. Action can seem somehow passive.[19]

So the phenomenon of willing to do something, which is so much part of our thinking about action, begins on examination to seem as mysterious as motive. At this point, you might suspect a kind of tension here. On the one hand, I place great emphasis on the importance of motive and character in our assessment of people – action isn't the only proper object of assessment. Yet, on the other hand, I'm admitting, or even insisting on, the opacity of the springs of action, of our motives, our will and our character.[20]

It's true, there is a tension here. But I think this tension is true to life, true of life. Motive and character *are* central to our thinking, and yet they *are* so often opaque to us. And think how dull life would be if we could neatly predict what others – and we ourselves – will do, with the certainty that we have about the movements of the planets. We are all of us round characters, and round characters surprise us by definition: 'The test of a round character is whether it is capable of surprising in a convincing way. If it never surprises, it is flat. If it does not convince, it is flat pretending to be round.' A round character 'has the incalculability of life about it'.[21]

The main practical lesson to be learned from this is that we should be circumspect about our own motives and character traits. Circumspection has two meanings in the Oxford English Dictionary; it's the second that I'm after: 'circumspect action or conduct; attention to circumstances that may affect an action or decision; caution, care, heedfulness, circumspectness'. Circumspection in this sense is, like strength of will, a kind of executive virtue.

On Personality

CIRCUMSPECTION AND FORWARD PLANNING: ODYSSEUS AND ALYPIUS

If we can't be sure of our own motivations, or of our character, if many of the real springs of action are beyond our conscious awareness, then we would do well to realise this in advance of the moment of action, and to plan accordingly. Thus the deployment of the executive virtue of circumspection in forward planning comes temporally prior to strength of will. Without the proper circumspection about our motives and character, strength of will can both be not enough and come too late.

Odysseus, resourceful Odysseus, was, of course, the master of this kind of forward planning. And it is exemplified in his dealing with the Sirens. He did have the benefit of being forewarned by Circe:

> You will come first of all to the Sirens, who are enchanters
> of all mankind and whoever comes their way; and that man
> who unsuspecting approaches them, and listens to the Sirens
> singing, has no prospect of coming home and delighting
> his wife and little children as they stand about him in greeting,
> but the Sirens by the melody of their singing enchant him.
> They sit in their meadow, but the beach before it is piled with boneheaps
> of men now rotted away, and the skins shrivel upon them.
> You must drive straight on past, but melt down sweet wax of honey
> and with it stop your companions' ears, so none can listen;
> the rest, that is, but if you yourself are wanting to hear them,
> then have them tie you hand and foot on the fast ship, standing
> upright against the mast with the ropes' ends lashed around it,
> so that you can have joy in hearing the song of the Sirens;

> but if you supplicate your men and implore them to set you
> free, then they must tie you fast with even more lashings.[22]

And this is just what Odysseus did:

> So they sang, in sweet utterance, and the heart within me
> desired to listen, and I signalled to my companions to set me
> free, nodding with my brows, but they leaned on and rowed
> hard,
> and Perimedes and Eurylochos, rising up, straightaway
> fastened me with even more lashings and squeezed me
> tighter.[23]

Like Odysseus, it can make sense to be circumspect, by plot-ting against your future self, by putting things in your way to prevent your acting out of temptation.[24] In the film *Disclosure*, the Michael Douglas character lacked circumspection: he let himself get into a situation where he was highly likely to become sexually compromised by the Demi Moore character, the woman who has just been appointed as his new boss, and with whom he had an affair before he got married. He should have kept out of her way that evening in the office, after everyone else had gone home. Another example: being less than fully temperate, there's a risk that you'll be tempted if there's a bar of chocolate in the fridge last thing at night. Then make sure that there isn't any there! Keep out of the way of temptation, and keep temptation out of the way of you!

There's an interesting implication of this. If you are cir-cumspect about your motives and character traits, as I say you should be, you won't consider yourself to be fully virtuous – not wholly and completely reliable in your actions, even (in that telling expression) with the best will in the world. You'll acknowledge that you're likely to be tempted in ways that the

On Personality

fully virtuous person wouldn't be. So, somewhat ironically, even if you identify with your trait, and aspire to be as close to being fully virtuous as possible, it is a mistake to ask yourself, in thinking about what is the right thing to do, 'What would the virtuous person do here?' For the *really* virtuous person wouldn't be tempted by the Sirens, by the Demi Moore character, by the chocolate in the fridge, and could therefore blithely go into these situations, in which the rest of us would be tempted. The better question to ask is, 'What would the virtuous person *advise* me to do here?' The virtuous person may well wisely advise you to be circumspect, and, like Odysseus, to take steps in advance to prevent yourself from doing what you will be tempted to do.[25]

Lack of circumspection is exemplified by Alypius: St Augustine tells us about him in his *Confessions*. Alypius and Augustine were friends in Carthage, where Alypius was carried away by 'the whirlpool of Carthaginian morals', and became 'sucked into the folly of the circus games'. But he started to attend Augustine's lessons. Hearing Augustine speak, about weakness and the folly of the games, 'he jumped out of the deep pit in which he was sinking by his own choice and where he was blinded by an astonishing pleasure. With strict self-control he gave his mind a shaking, and all the filth of the circus games dropped away from him, and he stopped going to them.'

Later, Alypius left for Rome, before Augustine did, to study law. Now this is where Alypius failed to be circumspect about his own character and strength of will. Augustine tells us what happened, and it's worth quoting in full, for we're in the hands of a great psychologist:

He [Alypius] held such spectacles in aversion and detestation;

but some of his friends and fellow-pupils on their way back from a dinner happened to meet him in the street and, despite his energetic refusal and resistance, used friendly violence to take him into the amphitheatre during the days of the cruel and murderous games. He said: 'If you drag my body to that place and sit me down there, do not imagine you can turn my mind and my eyes to those spectacles. I shall be as one not there, and so I shall overcome both you and the games.' They heard him, but none the less took him with them, wanting perhaps to discover whether he could actually carry it off. When they arrived and had found seats where they could, the entire place seethed with the most monstrous delight in the cruelty. He kept his eyes shut and forbade his mind to think about such fearful evils. Would that he had blocked his ears as well! A man fell in combat. A great roar from the entire crowd struck him with such vehemence that he was overcome by curiosity. Supposing himself strong enough to despise whatever he saw and to conquer it, he opened his eyes. He was struck in the soul by a wound graver than the gladiator in his body, whose fall had caused the roar. The shouting entered by his ears and forced open his eyes. Thereby it was the means of wounding and striking to the ground a mind still more bold than strong, and the weaker for the reason that he presumed on himself when he ought to have relied on You. As soon as he saw the blood, he at once drank in savagery and did not turn away. His eyes were riveted. He imbibed madness. Without any awareness of what was happening to him, he found delight in the murderous contest and was inebriated by bloodthirsty pleasure. He was not now the person who had come in, but just one of the crowd which he had joined, and a true member of the group which had brought him.[26]

WHERE WE'VE GOT TO AND WHERE WE'RE GOING

I've put forward a case for it being right to reproach people, like the Captain, for their bad character traits, and to hold them directly responsible morally for being the way they are. But we're not right to reproach people for those of their traits that aren't reason-responsive.

Turning to Jim's motives and his character, though, we should be less sure of what to say. Was he insufficiently circumspect about his motives and character? Perhaps; he was certainly wrong to think himself to be 'unflinching as a hero in a book'. But Jim didn't have the advantage that Odysseus and Alypius had, of knowing in advance what was coming up. He was a 'victim' of circumstantial moral luck, and suddenly, without warning, the fateful moment was on him. Jim's big mistake, I think, was not what he did (although what he did was wrong); it was to ruin the rest of his life by obsessively reproaching himself for that one moment, and for refusing to see or to accept that others could love him for who he was, warts, weakness and all.

These reflections lead us to the final chapter: to a narrative conception of the self, one that involves seeing motivation and character in the round, as part of a personality that is developing and changing constantly over the course of a life. Any residual idea of personality traits as *fixed* will finally be put well and truly to rest. Let's give Marlow, my last great psychologist of this chapter, the final word. In trying to find an 'excuse' for Jim's conduct, he said, 'I see well enough now that I hoped for the impossible – for the laying of what is the most obstinate ghost of man's creation, of the uneasy doubt uprising like a mist, secret and gnawing like a worm, and more chilling than the certitude of death – the doubt of the sovereign power enthroned in a fixed standard of conduct' (p. 37).

Five

THE OUTSIDE AND INSIDE VIEWS

If you were someone who knew me when I was twenty, and you met me again today, you might say to me: 'Peter, how you've changed! You're totally different from the Peter Goldie that I knew so well.' For you to say that I've changed, or even that I'm 'totally different', isn't to say, of course, that I'm literally a different person, just as to say of a tomato that it's changed — it was firm and green and is now soft and red — isn't to say that it's literally a different tomato; rather, the very same tomato has different properties. So what you're saying about me is that I, the very same person that I was at twenty, have different properties. The different properties that you notice about me, not having seen me for such a long time, are changes in my personality traits, that is, in my dispositional properties: you notice that now I'm gloomy, whereas I used to be cheerful and sparky, and so on.

In contrast, living with yourself on a day-to-day basis, you tend to notice the way the world is changing, rather than the way you are changing, and if you do notice that you are changing, it's your changing occurrent thoughts and feelings that you'll notice, and not your changing personality traits. So, perhaps, living with yourself, your own personality traits won't even feature in your consciousness at all: perhaps there is just what William James has called the 'big blooming buzz and confusion' of the stream of consciousness,[1] a multiplicity of occurrent thoughts, feelings, emotions, memories, that crude talk of personality tries to capture in a single word. Let's call this the *Woolfian inside view*, named after Virginia Woolf.

Now, if it's like that for you from the inside, then it's surely like that for me from the inside too. So if you were to use your imagination to project yourself into my position, seeing the world as I see it, from the inside looking out, taking up in imagination my Woolfian inside view, perhaps my personality traits wouldn't appear in what you imagine either. Perhaps it's only because of failure of imagination, or lack of information, that you think of me, but not of yourself, in terms of personality traits.

With the fragility of character and personality being at the centre of so much of the discussion of the earlier chapters, you might at this point think that I'm going to accept these implications of the Woolfian inside view, and say that thinking of ourselves, and of others, as having personality traits, as being *disposed* to this or to that, is inevitably a crude kind of flattening out, and should be replaced (at least wherever possible) with particular occurrent motives, thoughts, feelings, emotions – fleeting, momentary states of consciousness.

I'll start by looking at this Woolfian inside view. I've no doubt that it captures much of what conscious experience is like. But I think it doesn't capture all of it. Another part of conscious experience – putting the idea cryptically – turns the Woolfian view inside-out. Here, you take a perspective on yourself *as another*, from the inside but as if from the outside, seeing yourself as others see you, as being a *certain sort of person*. And it's just here, in what I'll call the *Augustinian inside view*, that your own personality and character re-emerges. Your thoughts about, and emotional responses to, what you have done in the past, and what you plan or hope to do in the future, often depend on your seeing yourself in this way. So, for all their fragility, personality and character remain essential to your thinking about yourself.

Looking backwards on your past, and looking forwards to your future, are reflective ways of thinking. Sometimes we're more reflective than at other times: sometimes we look back on our whole life and respond to how we see it ('I should have spent more time with my family'), and sometimes we look forward and respond to the remains of our life ('I can see in front of me a life of happy retirement in Del Mar California'). This kind of thinking – often in Augustinian style, seeing yourself as another – is part of what's involved in having a narrative sense of yourself, in thinking of your life as a narrative. Whether they are about larger or smaller parts of our lives, these narratives that we think through, and tell about ourselves, can profoundly affect our lives and our personality. In fact, some philosophers even say that our lives *are* a narrative, and having a narrative sense of yourself is essential to being the very person you are. This, as we'll see, is a mistake.[2]

THE WOOLFIAN INSIDE VIEW: A MYRIAD IMPRESSIONS

So-called stream of consciousness writers like Virginia Woolf (and James Joyce in the final chapter of *Ulysses*) try to capture the stream of someone's conscious thoughts – what conscious experience is like – through a kind of interior monologue. In her essay 'Modern fiction', Virginia Woolf rails against the typical novel:

> But sometimes, more and more often as time goes by, we suspect a momentary doubt, a spasm of rebellion, as the

pages fill themselves in the customary way. Is life like this? Must novels be like this?

Look within and life, it seems, is very far from being 'like this'. Examine for a moment an ordinary mind on an ordinary day. The mind receives a myriad impressions – trivial, fantastic, evanescent, or engraved with the sharpness of steel. From all sides they come, an incessant shower of innumerable atoms; and as they fall, as they shape themselves into the life of Monday or Tuesday, the accent falls differently from of old; the moment of importance came not here but there; so that, if a writer were a free man and not a slave, if he could write what he chose, not what he must, if he could base his work upon his own feeling and not upon convention, there would be no plot, no comedy, no tragedy, no love interest or catastrophe in the accepted style, and perhaps not a single button sewn on as the Bond Street tailors would have it. Life is not a series of gig lamps symmetrically arranged; life is a luminous halo, a semi-transparent envelope surrounding us from the beginning of consciousness to the end. Is it not the task of the novelist to convey this varying, this unknown and uncircumscribed spirit, whatever aberration or complexity it may display, with as little mixture of the alien and external as possible? We are not pleading merely for courage and sincerity; we are suggesting that the proper stuff of fiction is a little other than custom would have us believe it.[3]

The Woolfian inside view, of the stream of consciousness, doesn't just involve consciousness of one's immediate surroundings. It also captures the constant, and seemingly unbidden, arising of thoughts, feelings, memories, about all sorts of things that are not immediate. Here is Lily, painting, in *To the Lighthouse*:

> And as she lost consciousness of outer things, and her name
> and her personality and her appearance, and whether
> Mr Carmichael was there or not, her mind kept throwing up
> from its depths, scenes, and names, and sayings, and
> memories and ideas, like a fountain spurting over that
> glaring, hideously difficult white space, while she modelled it
> with greens and blues.[4]

As I've already suggested, from this Woolfian inside view it might seem as if personality traits fade away, to be replaced by what 'personality' merely points towards – 'a myriad impressions', 'an incessant shower of innumerable atoms'. Or I could perhaps use an analogy that wasn't available to Woolf: when you look at a photographic image of a human face on a computer screen, you see eyes, nose, chin, mouth; but as you increase the magnification, all that remains is a pixillated mass of colours, with no discernible shapes; facial features as such have disappeared. And similarly, close up, from the Woolfian inside view, personality disappears. 'Not only was furniture confounded; there was scarcely anything left of body or mind by which one could say "This is he" or "This is she".'[5] 'She would not say of any one in the world now that they were this or were that . . . she would not say of Peter, she would not say of herself, I am this, I am that.'[6] The barrier between people and personalities disappears, merging into a shared consciousness, shared memories: 'and she felt, with her hand on the nursery door, that community of feeling with other people which emotion gives as if the walls of partition had become so thin that practically (the feeling was one of relief and happiness) it was all one stream, and chairs, tables, maps, were hers, were theirs, it did not matter whose'.[7]

Whether or not this evanescence of personality is what Woolf had in mind (and some of what she says suggests to me that it is), I think that our own personality *doesn't* disappear from the inside: it remains because it is an essential part of our lives as conscious beings, capable of reflecting, Augustinian style, on our own occurrent thoughts and feelings, and on our own personality traits – capable of thinking backwards, about who we were and what we did, and forwards, about who we think we ought to be, and what we plan, intend or hope to do. So let's look at the Augustinian inside view.

THE AUGUSTINIAN INSIDE VIEW: ONESELF AS ANOTHER

We've seen in earlier chapters that reflective consciousness involves the ability to think about our own psychological states. Sometimes, in reflective consciousness, we do more than that: sometimes we also approve or disapprove of our thoughts and feelings and psychological dispositions, and we think how they might be changed, hopefully for the better.

This is very much part of what it is to be a human. St Augustine's account of his conversion, in his *Confessions*, captures the idea with unique brilliance. Not only does he want to be other than the way he is, he wants to *want* to be other than the way he is: he recognises his own badness and is striving to want to change in spite of his own resistance.[8] What we find in the *Confessions* is a kind of thinking that is different from – and complementary to – the Woolfian inside view. Augustine sees himself as another, and directs his thoughts to himself (sometimes via God), so that what is taking place is not an inner Woolfian *monologue* but an inner Augustinian *dialogue*, between that part of him that still wants to enjoy the pleasures of the flesh, and that part of him that wants to change for the better and wants to *want* to change for the better; recall his famous prayer, 'Grant me chastity and continence, but not yet.' Throughout the *Confessions*, but especially in the moments leading up to his conversion, we have passages such as these:

> You took me up from behind my own back where I had placed myself because I did not wish to observe myself and you set me before my face so that I should see how vile I was . . . But the day had now come when I stood naked to myself . . . I was gnawing at my inner self . . . With what verbal rods did I not scourge my soul so that it would follow me in my attempt to go after you! . . . But my madness with myself was part of the process of recovering health . . . Such was my sickness and my torture as I accused myself even more bitterly than usual . . . Inwardly I said to myself: Let it be now, let it be now. Vain trifles and the triviality of the empty-headed . . . tugged at the garment of my flesh and whispered 'Are you getting rid of us?' This debate in my heart was a struggle of myself against myself . . . From a hidden depth a profound self-examination had dredged up a heap of all my misery and set it 'in the sight of my heart' . . . For I felt my past to have a grip on me. It uttered wretched cries: 'How long, how long is it to be?' 'Tomorrow, tomorrow.' 'Why not now? Why not an end to my impure life in this very hour?'[9]

In Augustine, in this particularly reflectively conscious human being, past, present and future come together: he sees the way he has been, and the way he is, and he feels guilty and ashamed of it; and he sees how it is possible to change, to change into a better person. What Augustine recognised, and was ashamed of, was the long-term dispositional structure of his motivations: his lack of chastity and continence, the profligate life he had led in the past. Whilst each particular wrong act would have its own particular motives, these motives were expressions of what he recognised and was ashamed of – his *character*. For Augustine, the very possibility of reform, of conversion, was predicated on his seeing his past actions in this light, and not, for example, as excusable aberrations. The effort to change – to become a different person – must be based on being able to look back on your past in this way, and to see that a change in *disposition* is needed. (There are comparisons to be made here between the Augustinian inner dialogue with a better self, and the Freudian notion of the super-ego, the internalised parental figure. But they are just comparisons; I wouldn't want Augustine to turn into a kind of proto-Freud.)

After his conversion, in setting himself a course to abandon his past ways, in plotting his future life, he wasn't just making a *prediction* of what he would do, he was *avowing* what he would do; this is what's involved in making a commitment. Of course, conversions don't happen often in our life, if at all. But the Augustinian inner dialogue extends beyond conversions and attempted conversions. It extends more generally and widely to the ways in which we can look forwards and look backwards on our life, where we sometimes need to see ourselves from the outside, as having personality traits. Considering this will lead me to autobiographical narrative, and to the narrative sense of self.

PLANS AND COMMITMENTS

We make plans and commitments with other people: we agree to meet at the Rat and Parrot at 7 pm; we promise to be home by 10 pm. This is very common: we each make something like ten joint plans every day.[10] Also, like Augustine, we commonly make plans and commitments *with ourselves*, in an inner dialogue. We even sometimes talk to ourselves in the second person (for a dialogue does involve a 'second person'): urging ourselves on, telling ourselves not to forget someone's birthday, making mental lists of things to do, running through a mental diary of the week ahead, resolving to change, promising a treat to ourselves, and so on: 'Come on you fool, get on with it, stop fiddling about! If you work hard this morning and get enough done, you can allow yourself a glass of wine at lunchtime, and then go and buy that suit.'

It's often discussed by philosophers what the medium of thinking is: is it linguistic, imagistic, or what? I think it was J. M. Keynes, the famous Cambridge economist, who was once asked whether he thought in words or in pictures, and he replied that he thought in thoughts. This is a nice remark, and surely just right. But the idea I have here is that this kind of thinking, the kind that is involved in an inner Augustinian dialogue, is, of all kinds of thinking, the closest to thinking in words – to what is in effect thinking out loud to ourselves (and sometimes that is *just* what we do). Putting it another way, at times like this, one's thoughts, often accompanied by physical expression of emotion – a stamp of the foot, a clenching of the jaw – are closest to actual verbal expression.

What's all this got to do with personality? A lot. Imagine for a moment that the dialogue is actually with another person. In admonishing someone else, urging him on, counselling him, reminding him, telling him not to forget something, you ought to take account of what sort of person he is. Does he need to be reminded about her birthday? Well, is he the forgetful type? Is it a good idea to promise her a treat if she does her tax return? Well, is she the sort of person who responds to carrots or to sticks? The same principle applies to the Augustinian inner dialogue: you, your better, wiser, more reflective self, often needs to take account of the sort of person you are, with all your foibles and weaknesses, in order to advise, counsel, form plans, intentions and so on. Should I plan to go to the Rat and Parrot and then do some work when I get home? Well, am I someone who is inclined to work after a couple of beers?

Sometimes this planning involves circumspection, recognising and taking account of the fact that your traits are not as robust (stable and cross-situationally reliable) as you would like them to be. Can I rely on myself to withstand the temptations of the offer of the third glass of champagne, as I know I should? Well, maybe not, so I should make plans to leave the party before the offer is made (pre-book a taxi perhaps, and thereby, like Odysseus, have my hands tied). Being circumspect in this way – doubting your own reliability of character and personality – is, ironically, a form of self-knowledge; conversely, believing you are reliable when you are not is a form of ignorance.

Not all forming of intentions and plans involves us in Augustinian style reflection. Plans and intentions are often structured in a kind of hierarchical fashion, like a family tree, with the 'larger' plans generating a range of further plans and intentions, each of these generating yet further plans, and so on. For example, the larger plan, to spend more time with your family, might generate, amongst others, a plan to go on a family holiday; the plan to go on holiday generates a plan to go to Bali; this plan generates a plan to go shopping for a new swimsuit; and so on. And it's when you deliberate about the larger plans that you will typically be more likely to engage in Augustinian reflectiveness, reflectively seeing yourself as you now are, and as you could be, from a perspective in which you yourself feature. Maybe it was as a result of coming to see yourself as a workaholic, and thinking badly of yourself for it, that you came to form the plan to be more of a family person. On another occasion, the causality might go in the other direction, from forming a plan to seeing yourself Augustinian style in the future: planning to be more of a family person might lead to your seeing yourself in the future as a loving parent of your children, as you once were.

We differ individually in the manner and extent of our reflectiveness about our own lives; being a reflective person is a personality trait. Some might reflect, Augustinian style, on the smallest matters; others might never stop to think about how much they've changed over the years. And it's easy to see the dangers for the unreflective person: one can drift into a way of life without realising what kind of person one has become.

What's now beginning to emerge is the connection between Augustinian style thinking and narrative: autobiographical narrative thinking, and having a narrative sense of self. So let's now explore this.

NARRATIVES AND LIVES

What is a narrative? It's generally accepted (amongst so-called narratologists) that a minimal feature of any narrative is that it should reveal causal connections between the actions and events that are portrayed in a way which a list, or an annal, or a chronicle (in the words of Elbert Hubbard, just one damn thing after another) would fail to do. E. M. Forster's example of something less than a narrative is 'The king died and then the queen died.' This sentence implies that the queen's dying was a later event than the king's dying, but it is silent about whether the earlier event caused the later one. So it's less than a narrative. Whereas 'The king died, and then the queen died of grief' does reveal the causal connection between the two events: 'the sense of causality overshadows it'.[11]

With just this minimal feature, one can have a narrative of, for example, the first few seconds of big bang. But when we come to 'people-narratives', by which I mean simply narratives in which people feature as people (and not, for example, as objects for scientific investigation), the narrative should also present what happened in a way that enables the audience or the reader to make sense of the thoughts, feelings and actions of those people who are internal to the narrative. In Forster's very simple example of a people-narrative, we can readily appreciate, find intelligible, the thoughts and feelings that could go on in someone's mind on the death of someone they love, and how those thoughts and feelings could lead to that person's death, out of grief.

Now Forster, as we've seen, placed great emphasis, rightly so, on the importance of characters in narratives (from now on it's only people-narratives that I have in mind): character, action and the way the narrative unfolds are intimately related. As Henry James said:

> What is character but the determination of incident? What is incident but the illustration of character? . . . It is an incident for a woman to stand up with her hand resting on a table and to look out at you in a certain way; or if it be not an incident I think it will be hard to say what it is. At the same time it is an expression of character.[12]

'Character' in this sense picks out individuals with personality traits that distinguish them from others; it needn't pick out flat characters, types, caricatures. And it's because of this

individuality that each particular character 'determines incident' in a way that another character would not. The narrative
of Michael Ondaatje's beautifully crafted The English Patient
wouldn't have turned out as it did if the central characters had
been different. The transition in South Africa from apartheid
wouldn't have happened with so little bloodshed if Nelson
Mandela had been a vindictive, vengeful man. Conversely,
someone's character and personality, expressed and revealed
in action, are themselves shaped by the 'incidents' in which
he or she is involved.[13] In Mystic River, a film directed by Clint
Eastwood (based on a book by Dennis Lehane), the character
and personality of three men, who grew up together in a poor
district of Boston, were shaped by the sheer contingency of a
single incident: of the three of them, kids playing in the street,
just one was abducted in a car and subjected to several days of
sexual abuse before managing to escape. The other two knew
that it could so easily have been them instead, and, if it had,
how differently they, and their lives, would have turned out.

When we look backwards or forwards on our lives, we
often think in the form of a narrative: character and incident
together. Like plans, these narratives can be 'larger' or 'smaller',
structured hierarchically, from a narrative about a whole life,
right down to the 'mini-narrative' that you might tell of how
this morning you got up, got dressed and had breakfast.
Also, like plans, the larger narratives often involve seeing
yourself Augustinian style, as being a certain kind of person: a
loser like Marilyn Monroe's Sugar Kane in Some Like It Hot; a
loner like the James Coburn character in The Magnificent Seven; a
lover like Jack Nicholson in Carnal Knowledge.[14] In seeing yourself as you now are, you might or might not identify with
being this kind of person. If you don't, and if as a result
you make plans and commitments to change into a type that

you do identify with, the vicissitudes of life might see to it that you fail to achieve this ('the best laid schemes of mice and men . . .'). We can't always make our lives fall into the neat patterns of narrative genre-types, comforting as it is to think that we can. Nonetheless, the narratives that we weave about our lives can profoundly affect how we respond to our past, and how we lead our lives in the future: in an Augustinian dialogue, we can at least try to make our lives correspond to the stories that we tell ourselves about how our lives should go.

THE NARRATIVE SENSE OF SELF

This is where we come to the narrative sense of self. In auto-biographical narrative thinking, in looking back, in looking forward, our past or future selves feature as characters internal to the narrative, and we – the present, past-narrating we, or the present, future-planning we – are thereby in a position to take an evaluative perspective on our past or future selves, to evaluate our past or future actions, motives, character and personality (and that of other people too), and to arrive at a correlative emotional response. 'Damn it, I'm such a fool! I did a really stupid thing last week'; 'I see now that what I did, although it seemed right at the time, was mean and thoughtless: I won't do it again'; 'I'm fed up with being a drifter: I'm going to get my life organised.' This kind of thinking is what's involved in having a narrative sense of self.

Having a narrative sense of self isn't always an easy achievement. There is, of course, the extraordinary phenom-enon of Multiple Personality Disorder (MPD), in which, as Daniel Dennett puts it, 'a single human body *seems* to be shared by several selves, each, typically, with a proper name and an autobiography'.[15] But I want to focus on something else, still unusual, but less so. It's losing a sense of who you are, or what's sometimes called 'having an identity crisis'. This doesn't involve forgetting your proper name, your address, where you were born and brought up; your memory can be unimpaired. Rather, you can't *make sense* of your memories, of your past life, of who you now are. Let me explain.[16]

Sometimes, especially where what you remember was in some way tragic or traumatic – the death of a loved one, being fired from your job, accidentally maiming a child in a road accident, intentionally doing great harm to someone you love, divorce, the loss of a limb – you can't respond emotionally as you should; you're locked into the past, struggling to find some way out other than repetition. You remember it, you can give a 'matter-of-fact' explanation of what happened, and yet the narrative fails in some way to satisfy. It doesn't succeed. Something is lacking.

What is lacking in this kind of crisis is your ability to develop and maintain a narrative sense of self, at least so far as this part of your life is concerned: there is a single self with a single autobiography (no MPD), but you have no evaluative emotional response to what happened from the perspective that is essential to narrative thinking. Looking back on what happened, you might now feel emotions such as shock, puzzlement, horror, anger, surprise or just numbness, but these emotions are little more than a faint 'echo' of the response that you felt at the time. Your unsuccessful efforts to relate what happened as a satisfying narrative, perhaps by going over and over it in your mind, express a desire, a desire for what I'll call *emotional closure*. You want to, but can't, evaluate and respond emotionally to your past actions as you think you ought – perhaps with anger or forgiveness, perhaps with shame or regret, perhaps accepting that you were then a heartless bastard, a drunk, a dupe, a drifter, an obsessive workaholic. It's in this sense that, in remembering something, you sometimes ask yourself how you should think and feel about what you did or about what happened, realising perhaps that an answer is not readily available, and won't be forthcoming until you can see the past, and your past self, in what is rightly called 'the proper perspective'.

So, being able to look back on the past with the proper perspective, and to narrate what happened in the right way, with the right emotional response, is part of what's involved in having a narrative sense of self. Of course, many parts of our lives are of little interest and are perhaps altogether lost to memory: there never will be, and never need be, a narrative about them. But our story-telling about our past life doesn't need to cover every single incident in a complete life to be a satisfying story – to be one that achieves emotional closure and gives us a narrative sense of self.

TWO WORRIES: TRUTH AND OBJECTIVITY

So far, then, I've argued for the richness and importance of the idea of a narrative sense of self – a sense of self that embodies the Augustinian inner dialogue, self with self, seeing oneself as others do, and seeing one's character and personality – the sort of person one is – as developing and changing over time.

But worries begin to arise about this use of narrative. Narratives, you might think, are all very well when it comes to fiction, but they're deeply suspect in factual discourse, and especially in autobiographical discourse. For example, can't someone tell a story about her past that gives her 'emotional closure', that gets over the 'identity crisis', but that is still deeply in error? The desire for emotional closure can so easily transmute into self-deception, a desire for smug self-satisfaction, unwarranted vindication, or worse. We all know only too well of this possibility from our own lives, and our own sometimes rather desperate efforts (conscious and unconscious) to put our past actions in an unreasonably favourable perspective. These days it's called *spin*. If all we have are narratives, what grip is left on good old-fashioned notions like *truth* and *objectivity*? Let's take these worries in turn, with truth first.

THE WORRY ABOUT TRUTH

When we are concerned, as we are here, with factual narratives, we must distinguish two things: the factual narratives; and the facts, or what the factual narratives are about. Post-modernists are sometimes inclined to run these two things together ('there is nothing but the text'). But a narrative is distinct from what it is a narrative of. This might seem obvious, but it's surprisingly tempting to say more than this; I myself have been tempted in this direction, out of a desire to emphasise the importance of narrative in our lives.

The idea that lives, or parts of a life, have a 'narrative structure' is an ambiguous expression. In one sense, we might take it to mean that a life is a narrative. Alasdair MacIntyre, far from being a post-modernist, talks of 'lived narratives': 'What I have called a history is an enacted dramatic narrative in which the characters are also the authors.'[17] This is misleading. The right way to understand the idea that lives have a narrative structure is to see that lives, and parts of lives, unfold in a characteristic way which can be related in the form of a narrative (but which aren't themselves narratives).

Consider the characteristic ways in which human emotions unfold in response to the vicissitudes of human experience.

On Personality

There's the lost-and-found experience: you lose your keys; you look for them; you finally find them. For such a sequence of experiences there is a characteristic unfolding pattern of emotions: irritation; frustration; relief. And, for such a pattern of emotional experience, there is a characteristic narrative form: the story of something being lost (or stolen), a search, and, sometimes, a happy ending, when what is lost is finally found: *Raising Arizona*; *Bicycle Thieves*; or, at the level of a mini-narrative, Homer Simpson going to the fridge for a beer and finding none there – Doh! There's the experience of being wronged, becoming angry and seeking revenge, and, again, there is a characteristic narrative form: *Gladiator*; *Unforgiven*. There's the boy-meets-girl-and-lives-happily-ever-after experience; and so on, across the gamut of human experience and emotion. In a way, it would be more accurate to say, not that lives have a narrative structure, but that narratives have a life-like structure – narrative types or genres track how lives often go.

However, the denial that our lives are *literally* narratives, or that we are *literally* authors of our lives, doesn't imply that narratives, and our narrative sense of ourselves, aren't centrally important to how we lead our lives. As we've already seen, we think, talk and write *about* our lives as narratives, and our doing this can profoundly affect our lives as such, in our engagement with, and emotional response to, our past lives and who we were, and in our thinking and planning and hoping about the future and about what sort of person we want to be. We saw this with St Augustine: seeing himself as vile, and his past life as trivial, and responding emotionally to what he saw, led him to his conversion. Narrative thought and talk about our lives, or segments of our lives, can thus be embedded in, and profoundly influence, the lives that we lead, even though those lives aren't themselves narratives.

Once we've done this groundwork, separating out factual narratives and what factual narratives are about, the possibility of truth in factual narratives, as contrasted with fictional narratives, becomes relatively straightforward (leaving to one side the contentious question of what truth *is*). Roughly, a proposition in a narrative will be true if it corresponds to the facts. Thus, if I say that I didn't steal the sweets, what I say will be true just if things were, in fact, as I say they were. Contrary to the post-modern idea ('nothing but the text'), if others say that I did steal the sweets, there's no need to retreat to some 'meta-narrative' in order to arbitrate between the two competing narratives. Rather, there are two metaphysically distinct things here – language, which we use for describing the world, and the world; and what we say when we describe the world will be true or false depending on the way the world is. And these days we have a nicely accurate expression for those whose autobiographical narratives don't match up to the way the world is: we say that they need a reality check.

THE WORRY ABOUT OBJECTIVITY

Even if we can deal with the worry about truth in autobiographical factual narratives, there remains the worry about objectivity. I could relate to you a story of some aspect of my past life which is true, but nevertheless lacks objectivity: each proposition in the narrative, taken on its own, could be true, but you feel the whole story is somehow distorting; you feel that I've selectively and misleadingly left certain facts out, put other facts in, embellished, downplayed, put the best gloss on what happened, and so forth. Consider, analogously, how a government department might set out to 'present' last year's crime statistics: they take great care to state only what is true, but still, we feel, it's not objective; it's been *spun*.

An extreme response here is to dismiss *all* narratives as distorting, because all narratives are, as I've said, related from a perspective – that of the narrator. But that's wrong: there's nothing in the notion of a perspective that necessarily implies distortion, as if the only way we can be objective is to retreat like Charles Dickens' Gradgrind, to 'the facts'. We want, rather, to distinguish between those narratives and perspectives that are distorting and those that aren't.

Let's begin by turning our attention away from the narrator, me let's say, and towards the audience, you. You have a double interpretive task: you need to interpret the content of the narrative – what my story is about; and you need to interpret my act of narration itself. In relation to the second task, you might ask yourself this question: 'Why is he relating to me this particular narrative at this particular time, in this particular way?' Even if the narrative is given in response to a request ('What happened next?'; 'Why did you do that?'), it's still a legitimate question for you to ask why I am relating this narrative at this time in this way. Relating a narrative is, after all, just a kind of action, done for reasons. Thus, an audience can seek an explanation of why someone relates a narrative just as we can seek an explanation of other kinds of action.

In seeking such an explanation, you should look more widely than just to my own reasons, my own occurrent thoughts and feelings, that will explain my saying what I did. For, as we saw in Chapter 1, and in later chapters, we often classify someone's action and motives according to how we evaluate them, and not by reference to his or her reasons *as such*. Remember vain Arnold in the gym: we call his action vain without suggesting that he was motivated by vanity as such. Just the same principles apply to explaining an act of narration. Let's assume that I'm relating a narrative to you of how I was chosen for a much sought-after post in government. I might intend simply to 'tell it how it is', but still I might unintentionally reveal my vanity: my action – my act of narration – is expressive of reasons that can be appropriately classified as boastful and vain, even though it was no part of my intention to boast in telling you about my achievement.

What we have here is a divergence in evaluation, a divergence in perspective, between us: between me as narrator, and you as audience. I evaluate my getting the job as a palpable success, so pride on my part, and admiration on yours, are the appropriate responses. You, on the other hand, see my achievement in a less flattering light, and evaluate my act of narration as one expressive of boastful vanity.

So an audience isn't bound to accept as 'objective' the narrator's evaluation of, and perspective on, what happened. Indeed, a moment's reflection on the phenomenology of narrative discourse reveals how often we withhold acceptance: our evaluation of what happened often diverges from the narrator's. We are always free to come to a different evaluation of the narrated events, to take a different perspective, and we often take advantage of this freedom, as, analogously, we so often do when presented with government statistics: we accept the bare truth of what we're told, but we reject the spin.[18]

Consider a marital dispute, with diverging narratives about what happened, even though both narratives are true, as far as they go. You are asked to listen to both sides, and to come up with the right or appropriate narrative – an account that is both true *and* objective. In doing this, you try to glean the motivations of husband and wife in telling their stories as they do, and you then interpret these motivations as potentially expressive of their individual personalities and character. You then evaluate these individual motives and personalities to help you to arrive at the right or appropriate narrative of the dispute. This is, in large part, an ethical activity, and there's no universal formula or general rule for coming up with a right answer, any more than there is in ethics generally. Again we return to Aristotle's remark, suitably adapted: the virtuous person will tell a story at the right times, about the right things, towards the right people, and in the right way; and such a story will give rise to the right emotions and feelings.

And this remark reveals a further complication – one that is very important. Being, like most of us, less than fully virtuous, you should be circumspect about your own character and motives, so you can't just blithely assume, in your interpretations and evaluations, that you yourself are objective or free of bias – perhaps your 'take' on things also lacks objectivity and is distorting. With the best will in the world, you might unknowingly be influenced in your interpretation by some aspect of your personality of which you are unaware – repressed envy, unconscious sexual desire for someone, jealousy, love. So it is not as though you can be sure that, to quote a remark of Nietzsche's, 'reality stood unveiled before you only, and you yourselves were perhaps the best part of it'.[19]

NARRATIVE AND PERSONALITY

I can now develop something that I've hinted at in the last few paragraphs: the intimate connection between narrative and personality. The idea is this. Quite generally, as we've seen throughout this book, our thoughts and feelings, and the things that we do, can express or reveal our personality and character: her kind thoughts and actions express her kindness; his thoughts and actions in the gym express his vanity. Similarly, the ways we tell the story of our and other people's lives reflect, and are expressive of, our individual personalities.

To see how this works, let's start with literary style and how a writer can express her personality in a literary work. A literary style is, as the philosopher Jenefer Robinson has argued, 'a way of *doing* certain things, such as describing characters, commenting on the action and manipulating the plot'.[20] Thus, quoting Robinson again, 'we say that Jane Austen has a *style* of describing social pretension, because she consistently describes social pretension in an *ironic* way and the way she describes social pretension is expressive of a particular feature of her outlook, namely her irony'.[21]

Now, what I'm suggesting here is that just this idea can be applied to the way in which we each relate, or think about, our own or other people's lives. Say last month I fell over and broke my leg, and now I'm telling you what happened to me. I could tell this story in all sorts of ways, each one of which could be true: I could tell it as a light-hearted ironic comedy, a tragedy, a bleak comedy in the Mike Leigh manner, and so on. My choice of genre (whether an intentional choice or not), as well as what I put in the story, what I leave out, my tone of voice, the way I tell it – all this is expressive of, and reveals, my character and personality – just as my ostentatious way of dressing or my way of decorating my living room expresses my personality, and just as the government department expresses its arrogance and complacency in the way it presents the crime statistics.

Similarly, the stories that we tell about others – about our friends, relations and colleagues, and about politicians and others in the public arena – can be expressive of our personality. I typically downplay others' achievements; I do so because

On Personality

I'm an envious person. She characteristically tries to describe people in their most favourable light, and not to speak badly of their small mistakes and weaknesses; she's a generous person. He often spreads unfavourable rumours about colleagues and mutual acquaintances, and describes others' actions as if it's all part of a plot against him; he's spiteful, malicious and paranoid. These story-tellings are just a kind of action, which can be expressive of our personality, just like other kinds of action.

Not every aspect of the way I tell a story will reveal aspects of my personality. For example, if I need to hesitate in what I'm saying because I've got a stutter, my hesitation doesn't reveal a hesitant personality. If I'm inarticulate in what I say because I'm speaking in an unfamiliar language, this doesn't show that I'm an inarticulate person.

And there's one other wrinkle. Hugh might tell his story, of how he won the Best Actor Oscar, in a self-effacing way. This might be expressive of his self-effacing personality. But Hugh, an Englishman of a certain type let's say, might belong to a circle which is characteristically self-effacing in style. So there's a further question one might ask about Hugh: is he self-effacing *for that type of Englishman*? In other words, he might be more self-effacing than the average person, but he still might rightly be thought to be boastful in his circle. The parallels are clear: Pedro might be badly dressed *for an investment banker* but better dressed than most men; a Baroque sculptor might be austere in style *for a Baroque sculptor*, but florid compared to sculptors in general.

Our deeds, our facial features, our gestures, the clothes we wear, the CDs that we buy, the books we read, the friends that we choose to be with, the wallpaper we choose: all these and more can reveal, and be expressive of, our personality. And the same goes for what we say – for the stories that we tell about ourselves and others. By our stories shall we also be known.

WHERE WE'VE BEEN

This chapter, and the whole book, reveal a kind of tension in our thinking about personality and character (a different tension from the one I mentioned in Chapter 4). On the one hand, the closer one gets to people, the more evanescent personality seems, and the more fragile one's character; it seems that any attempt to reveal psychological dispositions (however fine-grained) will shiver into a mass of detail, into a Woolfian myriad impressions. And yet, on the other hand, talk of personality and character seems to be necessary in so many aspects of our lives: in making sense of, and predicting, what others and we ourselves will think, feel, do and say; in judging people morally; in seeing ourselves, as Augustine did, in a way that can allow us to change our ways, to change the kind of people we are; in developing a narrative sense of self; in seeing the stories that we tell, about ourselves and others, as expressive of our personality or character.

This tension (like the one in Chapter 4) is real, and shouldn't be explained away as some sort of illusion or fundamental mistake about personality and character. We are all round characters, but we need to flatten ourselves and others out a bit. The trick is in doing it the right way, and in being properly sensitive to the vicissitudes of personality, of character, of thought, feeling and action – of life.

ONE   THE PERVASIVENESS OF PERSONALITY

1 From Christopher Hibbert, *Nelson: A Personal History*, London: Penguin Books, 1994, pp. 101–2.

2 *Oxford English Dictionary*, Oxford: Oxford University Press, 2002.

3 In his *Aspects of the Novel*, London: Pelican Books, 1962.

4 Any good introductory book on social psychology will have a discussion of these and many other theories of personality; I have benefited from Robert Liebert and Michael Spiegler, *Personality: Strategies and Issues*, Pacific Grove, Calif.: Brooks/Cole Publishing, in many editions.

5 For a thorough discussion of these issues, see Rosalind Hursthouse's excellent *On Virtue Ethics*, Oxford: Oxford University Press, 1999, and Bernard Williams' 'Acting as the virtuous person acts', in Robert Heinaman, ed., *Aristotle and Moral Realism*, London: UCL Press, 1995, pp. 13–23.

6 *Hitler, vol. 1: 1889–1936: Hubris*, London: Penguin Books, 2001, p. 271.

7 Marcel Proust, *A la Recherche du temps perdu*, translated as *In Search of Lost Time*, C. K. Scott Moncrieff and T. Kilmartin, rev. D. J. Enright, London: Vintage Books, 1996, vol. 2, p. 565.

8 *Human All Too Human*, trans. R. J. Hollingdale, Cambridge: Cambridge University Press, 1986, Section 51. Incidentally, my example also reveals that having some personality traits depends on or requires having certain other things: to be a toff, it's necessary to have a certain amount of money and leisure time.

9 As evidenced by a recent poll in the United States: 84 per cent of adults interviewed believe that God performs miracles, and 48 per cent believe that they themselves have witnessed a miracle (*Newsweek* Poll conducted

by Princeton Survey Research Associates, 13–14 April 2000). I first read of this poll in 'Anti-Americans abroad' by Tony Judt, in the *New York Review of Books* 1, no. 7, 1 May 2003.

10 In one experiment in social psychology, people rated by observers as more attractive were also rated by those observers as having 'more socially desirable personality traits'; moreover, they were thought to be 'likely to secure more prestigious jobs than those of lesser attractiveness, as well as experiencing happier marriages, being better parents, and enjoying more fulfilling social and occupational lives'. See K. Dion, E. Berscheid and E. Walster, 'What is beautiful is good', *Journal of Personality and Social Psychology* 24, 1972, pp. 285–90. A recent study showed strong correlations of extraversion, conscientiousness and intelligence with various 'external attributes': 'face, voice, attire, gait, and overall appearance'; P. Borkenau and A. Liebler, 'Observable attributes as manifestations and cues of personality and intelligence', *Journal of Personality* 63, 1995, pp. 1–25.

11 In his *Eminent Victorians*, London: Chatto & Windus, 1918, p. 133.

12 There is a quite hard philosophical discussion of these issues by Robert Brandom in 'Non-inferential knowledge, perceptual experience, and secondary qualities', in Nicholas Smith, ed., *Reading McDowell on Mind and World*, London: Routledge, 2002, pp. 92–105.

TWO   GOOD AND BAD PEOPLE

1 'Character and will in modern ethics', in his *From Wodehouse to Wittgenstein: Essays*, Manchester: Carcanet, 1998, pp. 39–55. The citations are from pp. 39, 43 and 54–5. I am grateful to an anonymous reader for Routledge for referring me to this.

2 *Characters*, ed. and trans. J. Rusten, I. C. Cunningham and A. D. Knox, Cambridge, Mass.: Harvard University Press, 1993, pp. 95–7. This book had a significant influence on later Greek and Roman writing, and on writing in the Renaissance. Thanks to Adam Morton for telling me about this book.

3 Immanuel Kant, *Groundwork of the Metaphysics of Morals*, trans. H. J. Paton, New York: Harper Torchbooks, 1964, p. 394.

4 J. S. Mill, *Utilitarianism*, Chapter 2, paragraphs 19 and 20. Available in various editions.

5 David Hume, *A Treatise of Human Nature*, ed. L. A. Selby-Bigge, Oxford: Oxford University Press, 1978, p. 575.

6 *Nicomachean Ethics*, trans. Terence Irwin, Indianapolis: Hackett, 1985. Aristotle lists the first three conditions in one place (1105a27ff) and refers to the need for having the right feelings elsewhere, for example, 1099a16–20.

7 This second condition of Aristotle's is an especially difficult one to interpret. It would not be a satisfying interpretation if it turned out that a kind action must involve the person deciding – consciously – that they are doing a kind thing for its own sake. This would make virtuous action far too reflective and self-conscious. The interpretation that I prefer is the one put forward by Rosalind Hursthouse and Bernard Williams, which I referred to in note 5 of Chapter 1.

8 *Groundwork*, p. 416.

9 *Groundwork*, pp. 388–9.

10 Cited in H. J. Paton, *The Categorical Imperative: A Study in Kant's Moral Philosophy*, third edition, London: Hutchinson, 1958, p. 48.

11 Ithaca, NY: Cornell University Press, 1989.

12 David Hume, *Enquiries Concerning Human Understanding and Concerning the Principles of Morals*, ed. L. A. Selby-Bigge, Oxford: Oxford University Press, 1975, p. 270.

13 *On the Genealogy of Morals*, trans. Walter Kaufmann, New York: Vintage Books, 1967, Preface, Section 6.

14 This worry about circularity is closely related to what is sometimes called the Euthyphro dilemma, named after the dilemma posed by Socrates to Euthyphro in Plato's dialogue of that name: Socrates asked Euthyphro whether what is holy is holy because the Gods approve of it, or whether the Gods approve of it because it is holy.

15 *Enquiries*, p. 268.

16 *Enquiries*, p. 270.

17 For arguments along Aristotelian lines here, see Rosalind Hursthouse's *On Virtue Ethics*, Oxford: Oxford University Press, 1999, and Philippa Foot's *Natural Goodness*, Oxford: Clarendon Press, 2001.

18 *Nicomachean Ethics* 1106b20.

19 In his 'Virtue and reason', *Monist* 62, 1979, pp. 331–50, reprinted in a collection of his papers, *Mind, Value, and Reality*, Cambridge, Mass.: Harvard

University Press, 1998, pp. 50–73; the citation is from p. 51 of this volume.

20 Immanuel Kant, *The Metaphysics of Morals*, ed. and trans. M. Gregor, Cambridge: Cambridge University Press, 1996, 6: p. 384.

21 'Aristotle on learning to be good', in A. O. Rorty, ed., *Essays on Aristotle's Ethics*, Berkeley: University of California Press, pp. 69–92, at p. 78.

THREE   THE FRAGILITY OF CHARACTER

1 David Hume, 'Of National Character', in his *Essays, Moral, Political, and Literary*, Indianapolis: Liberty Fund, 1985, p. 197. Also available in various other editions.

2 I owe this way of putting it to Adam Morton.

3 Gilbert Harman, 'Moral philosophy meets social psychology', *Proceedings of the Aristotelian Society* 99, 1999, pp. 315–31, at p. 325. This, and many other kinds of bad reasoning that we are prone to, are discussed in R. Nisbett and L. Ross, *Human Inference: Strategies and Shortcomings of Social Judgement*, Englewood Cliffs, NJ: Prentice-Hall.

4 This bias is discussed, with references, by John Doris in his *Lack of Character: Personality and Moral Behaviour*, Cambridge: Cambridge University Press, 2002, pp. 97–8, to which I am greatly indebted in this chapter.

5 *Aspects of the Novel*, London: Pelican Books, 1962, p. 73.

6 There's also the boot-camp, *Full Metal Jacket*, kind of flattening out, but that's not my concern here.

7 *Aspects of the Novel*, p. 75.

8 *Human All Too Human*, trans. R. J. Hollingdale, Cambridge: Cambridge University Press, 1986, Section 160.

9 In his *Being and Nothingness*, trans. Hazel Barnes, London: Routledge, 1969, p. 64. Sartre's actual text has 'He's just a paederast.'

10 *Aspects of the Novel*, pp. 56–7.

11 L. Ross and R. Nisbett, *The Person and the Situation: Perspectives of Social Psychology*, New York: McGraw-Hill, 1991. The citations are from pp. 90, 120–1 and 124.

12 The first experiment was A. M. Isen and P. F. Levin, 'Effect of feeling good on helping: cookies and kindness', *Journal of Personality and Social Psychology* 21, 1972, pp. 384–8, and the second by J. M. Darley and C. D. Batson, ' "From Jerusalem to Jericho": a study of situational and dispositional variables in helping behaviour', *Journal of Personality and*

Social Psychology 27, 1973, pp. 100–8. These experiments, and others, are discussed at length in John Doris' book *Lack of Character*. In many ways the most famous experiment in this territory is one that I will not discuss: the experiments in obedience carried out by Stanley Milgram – see especially his *Obedience to Authority: An Experimental View*, New York: Harper and Row, 1974. I have several reasons for not discussing it here; one is that I've already discussed it in some detail in an earlier book, *The Emotions: A Philosophical Exploration*, Oxford: Clarendon Press, 2000.

13 These results are from P. Pietromonaco and R. E. Nisbett, 'Swimming upstream against the fundamental attribution error: subject's weak generalisations from the Darley and Batson study', *Social Behaviour and Personality* 10, 1982, pp. 1–4; they are reported in Ross and Nisbett's *The Person and the Situation*, p. 131, and in Doris' *Lack of Character*, p. 99.

14 'The nonexistence of character traits' was the title of a paper by Gilbert Harman, *Proceedings of the Aristotelian Society* 100, 2000, pp. 223–6. For further superficial impressions that Harman holds the extreme view, and also for the denial that this is what he really holds, see also his 'Moral philosophy meets social psychology', *Proceedings of the Aristotelian Society* 99, 1999, pp. 315–31.

15 *On Virtue Ethics*, Oxford: Oxford University Press, 1999, pp. 10, 11 and 12. Hursthouse does rightly admit that virtue is a matter of degree, and that people often have their 'blind spots' (p. 150). But it is the ideal that will concern me here.

16 This happened in 1595. News of the murders (the oldest child was 11) shocked England, and it was referred to by Shakespeare in *Henry IV Part 2*. Henry V, like Sultan Mehmet, is newly on the throne. Reminding his brothers that he doesn't have the same structure of motivations as the Sultan – that he is a different kind of person – Henry V spoke thus to them (referring to the Sultan as 'Amurath'): 'Brothers, you mix your sadness with some fear: This is the English, not the Turkish court; Not Amurath an Amurath succeeds, But Harry Harry.' The contemporary report, and the connection with *Henry IV Part 2*, are both in John Freely's *Inside the Seraglio: Private Lives of the Sultans in Istanbul*, London: Viking, 1999, p. 88.

17 I am very appreciative of Adam Morton's discussion of these matters in his *The Importance of Being Understood: Folk Psychology as Ethics*, London: Routledge, 2003.

18 Now we can see why Anthony Quinton (in Chapter 2) was mistaken to say that character just *is* strength of will. See Robert Roberts, 'Will power and the virtues', *The Philosophical Review* 93, 1984, pp. 227–47.

19 *Nicomachean Ethics* 1147b13 and 1147a20.

20 *Nicomachean Ethics* 1152a20.

21 *Nicomachean Ethics* 1151a25.

22 *Nicomachean Ethics* 1150a2 and 1145a30.

23 Kant criticised the ancient philosophers, and the Stoics in particular, for expecting too much of human beings: 'inasmuch as they represented the degree of virtue required by its pure law as fully attainable in this life, they strained the moral capacity of *human being*, under the name of a *sage*, far beyond the limits of his nature'. The references to these passages are as follows: *Religion with the Limits of Reason Alone*, p. 43; *The Metaphysics of Morals*, pp. 409, 446; the *Critique of Practical Reason* pp. 122 and 126–7.

FOUR   CHARACTER, RESPONSIBILITY AND CIRCUMSPECTION

1 *Lord Jim: A Tale*, Oxford World Classics, Oxford: Oxford University Press, 2002. All page references are to this edition. John Doris considers *Lord Jim* in his *Lack of Character* (Cambridge: Cambridge University Press, 2002), a book which I have mentioned several times already. His discussion is very helpful, and, although some of the lessons I draw from *Lord Jim* are different, I have benefited greatly from what Doris says.

2 In an interview with *The Guardian*, 19 July 2003.

3 For an excellent attack on this view, see Robert Merrihew Adams, 'Involuntary sins', *The Philosophical Review* 94, 1985, pp. 3–31, especially p. 12. The example that follows is an adaptation of one of Adams'. Generally, reading and thinking about this excellent paper has made me change my mind about these matters.

4 For a useful discussion of these issues, see Elliott Sober, 'Apportioning causal responsibility', *The Journal of Philosophy* 85, 1988, pp. 303–18. Thanks to Matteo Mameli for this reference.

5 Peter Strawson, 'Freedom and resentment', *Proceedings of the British Academy* 48, 1962, pp. 181–211. See also David Owen, *Reason without Freedom*, London: Routledge, 2000, and R. Jay Wallace, *Responsibility and the Moral Sentiments*, Cambridge, Mass.: Harvard University Press, 1998. There are

many other kinds of reactive attitudes we can have towards people's character traits. Notably (although they are not my concern here), many of them are aesthetic; see Colin McGinn's *Ethics, Evil, and Fiction*, Oxford: Clarendon Press, 1997, especially Chapter 5, 'Beauty of soul'.

6 There is a nice discussion of this in Adam Morton's *On Evil*, also in Routledge's Thinking in Action series.

7 I have been helped in what follows by David Owen's *Reason without Freedom*. There are subtle but important differences between the individual below-the-line reactive attitudes. In particular, perhaps blame as such is only felt towards someone's voluntary actions, and not towards their character. For discussion, see Adams' 'Involuntary sins', especially pp. 21–4. Thanks to Adam Morton for discussion.

8 Gilbert Harman, 'Moral relativism defended', *The Philosophical Review* 84, 1975, pp. 3–22. Harman does agree that we can say that what Hitler did was wrong.

9 'Involuntary sins', pp. 15 and 16.

10 See 'Involuntary sins', p. 17.

11 In this chapter, and especially over the last few pages, I have been influenced by Sabina Lovibond's *Ethical Formation*, Cambridge, Mass.: Harvard University Press, 2002, and by Susan Wolf's *Freedom within Reason*, New York: Oxford University Press, 1990.

12 This is discussed by John Doris in his *Lack of Character*, p. 90.

13 'Moral luck', in his *Mortal Questions*, Cambridge: Cambridge University Press, 1979. Kant discussed the idea in several places: for example in *The Metaphysics of Morals*, p. 392, in *Kant's Practical Philosophy*, trans. Mary Gregor, Cambridge: Cambridge University Press, 1996.

14 In his *Human All Too Human*, 'The wanderer and his shadow', Section 323, trans. R. J. Hollingdale, Cambridge: Cambridge University Press, 1986.

15 *Daybreak*, trans. R. J. Hollingdale, Cambridge: Cambridge University Press, 1982, Section 129.

16 See, for example, R. E. Nisbett and T. D. Wilson, 'The halo effect: evidence for unconscious alteration of judgements', *Journal of Personality and Social Psychology* 35, 1977, pp. 250–6; and 'The accuracy of verbal reports about the effects of stimuli on evaluations and behaviour', *Social Psychology* 41, 1978, pp. 18–31.

17 *Ecce Homo*, II, Section 9, in *On the Genealogy of Morals and Ecce Homo*, trans. Walter Kaufmann, New York: Vintage Books, 1967.

18 *Diaries 1899–1942*, trans. Philip Payne, New York: Basic Books, 1998; the citation is in Notebook II, p. 101.

19 In his great work *The Man without Qualities*, Musil, discussing the same example of turning over in bed, also suggests this passivity in action. He says, 'you decide on one move and then another, without doing anything; finally, you give up; and then all at once you've turned over! One really should say you've been turned over'; *The Man without Qualities*, trans. Sophie Wilkins, New York: Alfred A. Knopf, 1995, vol. 2, p. 801.

20 Kant, who, like me, placed such emphasis on motive, also thought that our motives were mysterious: 'For a human being cannot see into the depths of his own heart so as to be quite certain, in even a *single* action, of the purity of his moral intention and the sincerity of his disposition . . . In the case of any deed, it remains hidden from the agent himself how much pure moral content there has been in his disposition', *The Metaphysics of Morals*, p. 392.

21 *Aspects of the Novel*, p. 81.

22 *The Odyssey of Homer*, trans. and with an introduction by Richard Lattimore, New York: HarperCollins, 1975, Book XII, lines 39–54.

23 Lines 192–6.

24 There is an interesting book about all this: Jon Elster, *Ulysses and the Sirens: Studies in Rationality and Irrationality*, Cambridge: Cambridge University Press, 1979.

25 For discussion of the 'advice' and the 'example' or 'emulation' models, see Michael Smith, 'Internal reasons', *Philosophy and Phenomenological Research* 55, 1995, pp. 109–31. The advice model is also argued for by Doris. The question people sometimes ask is 'What would Jesus do?', and it's interesting in this context to note that Jesus was tempted.

26 *Confessions*, VI viii 13, pp. 100–1 of the Oxford World's Classics edition, trans. H. Chadwick, 1991.

FIVE PERSONALITY, NARRATIVE AND LIVING A LIFE

1 In 'Percept and concept: the import of concepts', in his *Some Problems of Philosophy*, 1996 reprint, Bison Books, from the original, New York: Longmans Green, 1911, p. 50.

2 Parts of this chapter were first developed in a recent paper of mine: 'One's remembered past: narrative thinking, emotion and the external

perspective', *Philosophical Papers* 32, 2003, pp. 301–19. I thank the editors of that journal.

3 'Modern fiction', in *The Common Reader*, vol. 1, ed. Andrew McNeillie, London: Hogarth Press, pp. 149–50. Keith Oatley, and some comments by Pam Joll, suggested to me the importance of Woolf's work here. Oatley uses the term 'Woolfian consciousness' in 'The narrative mode of consciousness and selfhood', in P. Zelazo and M. Moscovitch, eds., *Handbook of Consciousness*, Cambridge: Cambridge University Press, forthcoming.

4 *To the Lighthouse*, London: Penguin, 1964, p. 181.

5 *To the Lighthouse*, p. 144.

6 *Mrs Dalloway*, London: Grafton Books, pp. 9 and 10.

7 *To the Lighthouse*, p. 131.

8 The contemporary philosopher Harry Frankfurt has argued that the kind of 'second-order' wanting (wanting not to want something) is an essential part of what it is to be a person. See, for example, 'Freedom of the will and the concept of a person', reprinted in his *The Importance of What We Care About*, Cambridge: Cambridge University Press, 1988.

9 *Confessions*, the Oxford World's Classics edition, trans. H. Chadwick, 1991, extracts from Book VIII, pp. 133–54.

10 K. Oatley and J. Laroque, 'Everyday concepts of emotions following every-other-day errors in joint plans', in J. Russell, J.-M. Fernandez-Dols, A. S. R. Manstead and J. Wellenkamp, eds., *Everyday Conceptions of Emotions: An Introduction to the Psychology, Anthropology, and Linguistics of Emotion*, NATO ASI Series D 81, Dordrecht: Kluwer, 1995, pp. 145–65.

11 *Aspects of the Novel*, London: Pelican Books, 1962, p. 87. Forster uses the term 'story' for the first and 'plot' for the second. These terms are, I think, confusing in this context.

12 In 'The art of fiction', *Longman's Magazine*, September 1884, reprinted in *The Portable Henry James*, ed. M. D. Zabel, New York: Viking, pp. 391–418.

13 This is very clearly discussed in H. Porter Abbott's *The Cambridge Introduction to Narrative*, Cambridge: Cambridge University Press, 2002.

14 I am not a scholar of Carl Jung, but there are clear connections between these ideas and Jung's notion of the collective unconscious, with its archetypes.

15 In his *Consciousness Explained*, London: Penguin, 1991, p. 419.

16 David Velleman's recent work in this area has helped me. See a number of his excellent papers on his website:

http://www-personal.umich.edu/~velleman/

17 *After Virtue: A Study in Moral Theory*, London: Duckworth, 1981, p. 215. There is a helpful discussion of these issues by Sam Vice in 'Literature and the narrative self', *Philosophy* 78, 2003, pp. 93–108.

18 Charles Guignon has a very clear discussion of these issues in relation to psychotherapy in 'Narrative explanation in psychotherapy', *American Behavioural Scientist* 41, 1998, pp. 558–77.

19 *The Gay Science*, Book 2, Section 57.

20 Jenefer Robinson, 'Style and personality in the literary work', *The Philosophical Review* 94, 1985, pp. 227–47, at p. 227.

21 p. 230.

Index

THINKING IN ACTION – order more now

Available from all good bookshops

Credit card orders can be made on our **Customer Hotlines**:
UK/RoW: + (0) 8700 768 853
US/Canada: (1) 800 634 7064

Or buy online at: www.routledge.com

Routledge
Taylor & Francis Group

TITLE	AUTHOR	ISBN	BIND	Prices UK	US	CANADA
On Belief	Slavoj Zizek	0415255325	PB	£8.99	$14.95	$19.95
On Cosmopolitanism and Forgiveness	Jacques Derrida	0415227127	PB	£8.99	$14.95	$19.95
On Film	Stephen Mulhall	0415247969	PB	£8.99	$14.95	$19.95
On Being Authentic	Charles Guignon	0415261236	PB	£8.99	$14.95	$19.95
On Humour	Simon Critchley	0415251214	PB	£8.99	$14.95	$19.95
On Immigration and Refugees	Sir Michael Dummett	0415227089	PB	£8.99	$14.95	$19.95
On Anxiety	Renata Salecl	0415312760	PB	£8.99	$14.95	$19.95
On Literature	Hillis Miller	0415261252	PB	£8.99	$14.95	$19.95
On Religion	John D Caputo	041523333X	PB	£8.99	$14.95	$19.95
On Humanism	Richard Norman	0415305233	PB	£8.99	$14.95	$19.95
On Science	Brian Ridley	0415249805	PB	£8.99	$14.95	$19.95
On Stories	Richard Kearney	0415247985	PB	£8.99	$14.95	$19.95
On Personality	Peter Goldie	0415305144	PB	£8.99	$14.95	$19.95
On the Internet	Hubert Dreyfus	0415228077	PB	£8.99	$14.95	$19.95
On Evil	Adam Morton	0415305195	PB	£8.99	$14.95	$19.95
On the Meaning of Life	John Cottingham	0415248000	PB	£8.99	$14.95	$19.95
On Cloning	John Harris	0415317002	PB	£8.99	$14.95	$19.95

Contact our **Customer Hotlines** for details of postage
and packing charges where applicable.
All prices are subject to change
without notification.

...Big ideas to fit in your pocket